Magic

Unlock the Power of Natural Forces and Learn Techniques Such as Purification, Divination, Invocation, Astral Travel, Yoga and More

© Copyright 2020

This document is geared towards providing exact and reliable information regarding the topic and issue covered. The publication is sold with the idea that the publisher is not required to render accounting, officially permitted, or otherwise, qualified services. If advice is necessary, legal or professional, a practiced individual in the profession should be ordered from a Declaration of Principles which was accepted and approved equally by a Committee of the American Bar Association and a Committee of Publishers and Associations.

In no way is it legal to reproduce, duplicate, or transmit any part of this document in either electronic means or in printed format. Recording of this publication is strictly prohibited and any storage of this document is not allowed unless with written permission from the publisher. All rights reserved.

The information provided herein is stated to be truthful and consistent, in that any liability, in terms of inattention or otherwise, by any usage or abuse of any policies, processes, or directions contained within is the solitary and utter responsibility of the recipient reader. Under no circumstances will any legal responsibility or blame be held against the publisher for any reparation, damages, or monetary loss due to the information herein, either directly or indirectly.

Respective authors own all copyrights not held by the publisher.

The information herein is offered for informational purposes solely, and is universal as so. The presentation of the information is without contract or any type of guarantee assurance.

The trademarks that are used are without any consent, and the publication of the trademark is without permission or backing by the trademark owner. All trademarks and brands within this book are for clarifying purposes only and are owned by the owners themselves, not affiliated with this document.

Your Free Gift (only available for a limited time)

Thanks for getting this book! If you want to learn more about various spirituality topics, then join Mari Silva's community and get a free guided meditation MP3 for awakening your third eye. This guided meditation mp3 is designed to open and strengthen ones third eye so you can experience a higher state of consciousness. Simply visit the link below the image to get started.

https://spiritualityspot.com/meditation

Contents

INTRODUCTION 1
CHAPTER ONE: ACKNOWLEDGING THE MAGIC WITHIN 3
    THE GOAL OF MAGIC 5
    A RATIONAL EXPLANATION OF MAGIC 6
    MAGIC AND NLP 8
    THE POWER IS WITHIN YOU 9
CHAPTER TWO: MAGICAL LAW: DO WHAT YOU WILL 13
    DISCOVERING YOUR TRUE WILL: THE KEY TO TRANSFORMATION 13
    DISPELLING THE MYTHS SURROUNDING THE MAGICAL LAW 16
CHAPTER THREE: MEDITATION: THE POWER OF THE MIND 22
    MEDITATION: THE SKELETON KEY TO THE MAGICAL 23
    MEDITATION: THE ART OF MINDFULNESS 24
    MEDITATION TECHNIQUES 25
    WHY MEDITATE? 28
CHAPTER FOUR: YOGA: THE MAGIC OF THE PHYSICAL BODY 29
    SELF-DISCOVERY AND SELF REALIZATION THROUGH YOGA 29
    A BRIEF HISTORY OF YOGA 30
    MYSTICAL USES OF YOGA IN THE PAST 32
    YOGA ACCORDING TO ALEISTER CROWLEY 34
CHAPTER FIVE: MAGICAL ASTRAL TRAVEL TECHNIQUES 40
    WHAT IS ASTRAL PROJECTION? 40

WHY YOU SHOULD LEARN TO ASTRAL PROJECT	41
THE ASTRAL BODY	43
THE QABALAH AND THE TREE OF LIFE	44
ASTRAL PROJECTION METHODS	45
ASTRAL PROJECTION TECHNIQUES	46

CHAPTER SIX: BUILDING YOUR SACRED SPACE 51

YOUR ALTAR	51
CREATING YOUR ALTAR	52
CARE FOR YOUR ALTAR	54
CLEANSING YOUR ALTAR'S SPACE	55
WHAT TO DO WHEN THERE'S NO ROOM	56

CHAPTER SEVEN: THE TOOLS OF THE CRAFT 58

THE MOST POWERFUL TOOL OF ALL	65

CHAPTER EIGHT: PREPARING FOR RITUAL............................66

WHAT'S A RITUAL?	66
ELEMENTS AND COMPONENTS OF RITUALS	67
THE IMPORTANCE OF RITUALS	68
PREPARING FOR YOUR RITUAL	69
THE PROGRESSION OF THE RITUAL	70

CHAPTER NINE: PERFORMING PURIFICATION 73

PURIFICATION	73
BANISHING	74
STAYING CLEAN	75
CROWLEY'S LESSER BANISHING RITUAL OF THE PENTAGRAM	76
PREPARING FOR THE LESSER BANISHING RITUAL OF THE PENTAGRAM	77
THE PROCESS	78

CHAPTER TEN: THREE METHODS OF INVOCATION 80

CROWLEY'S THREE METHODS OF INVOCATION	81
ASSUMPTION OF GODFORMS	82

CHAPTER ELEVEN: THE ART OF DIVINATION.........................84

DIVINATION DEFINED	84
DIVINATION VS. FORTUNE TELLING	84
DIVINATION: SUBJECTIVE AND PERSONAL	85
PRACTICAL DIVINATION EXERCISES	85

CHAPTER TWELVE: MORE MAGICAL PRACTICES 91
    CONSECRATION 91
    EVOCATION 92
    MAGICAL FORMULAS 92
    MAGICAL RECORD 93
    MAGICAL WEAPONS 93
    MINERAL MAGIC 94
    STONES AND THEIR MAGICAL USES 94
CONCLUSION 99
VEA MÁS LIBROS ESCRITOS POR MARI SILVA 101
YOUR FREE GIFT (ONLY AVAILABLE FOR A LIMITED TIME) 102
REFERENCES 103

Introduction

What a curious choice you've made by reading this book. You're either a longtime practitioner of magic, or you're a beginner who's looking for guidance. Either way, you are reading this for a reason. Something has drawn you to this book, out of all the many others out there. So, stick with it.

You can skip to the areas that interest you most if you've been practicing magic for a while now. If you're a complete beginner, then it would be in your best interests to begin at the beginning.

You will find this work is unlike any other out there. It is up to date, very easy to understand, and will not leave you scratching your head about what's going on with each page. The exercises and methods found here are very simple to follow. That said, do not allow their simplicity to fool you, as they are ten times as powerful as they are simple.

Read this book on magic with an open mind and put everything you're about to learn into practice. What you will discover is a world full of magic and wonder, one in which you continue to live out your True Will, moment by moment. Imagine living a life where you are productive and grow in spirit and truth, whether you're awake or asleep.

Imagine understanding that the world around you brims with even more activity than you can perceive, and there are energies you can work with to sculpt the life meant for you and no one else. These are the treasures you're about to discover.

This text is not necessarily the last bus stop with all things magical, but it will offer you the most basic, useful, practical information that, when applied, will definitely pay off in huge ways! Highlight important sections, reread chapters of the book, and go off on a wonderful adventure as you explore the ideas in these pages when you're done.

By the time you're through, you will have learned so much, and if I've done my job right, you'll conclude that you have not learned enough... Nor could you ever. The whole point of this book is to give you what you need to set a fire in your soul and set you off and running on a quest to be more than you already are. It will help you express all the wonderful gifts that remain dormant in you and find that as far as the magical life and quest for knowledge go, there is no end. There is only more depth... and that is a wonderful thing, indeed.

Chapter One: Acknowledging the Magic Within

Let us begin our exploration of magic by getting into the etymology and origin of the word "magic." We will focus on magic in the context of the great Aleister Crowley's definitions, looking at it through the lens of his Thelema. Crowley was a mystic, a writer, and a ceremonial magician, a master of the most complex and elaborate rituals in magic.

Crowley developed the esoteric philosophy of The Thelema early in the 1900s. The word *thelema* has a simple yet potent meaning to the mystic who sees beyond the ordinary. It means "will." Or, if you prefer another way to put it:

- "To want"
- "To wish"
- "To will"
- "Purpose"

Without getting too into the *thelema* and off the subject of what you're interested in, lets wrap this up by clarifying the three key pillars that hold up the thelemic philosophy according to Crowley:

1. **"Do What Thou Wilt' Shall be the Whole of the Law."** In present-day English, that means "'Do what you will' shall be the whole of the Law." It is on you as the true follower of the Thelema to seek the path that resonates with you the most and follow it. This path is your True Will. It is your resonating moment by moment with nature. It is you fulfilling the highest calling for your soul.

2. **"Love is the Law, Love Under Will."** This means you must understand that at the very core of the Thelema is love. Love reigns, but it is only secondary to discovering what your true mission is and manifesting the your authentic destiny or will.

3. **"Every Man and Every Woman is a Star."** Just as every star in the universe has its own place in space, and just as every star is unique and unmistakably itself, so also is everyone on Earth. As a follower of the Thelema, understand that everyone has their own unique fingerprint, with their very own Wills, which they must fulfill. You have a path all your own, just like the cashier at Starbucks or the business executive looking pensively at his watch. Since everyone has their unique paths, there needn't be any conflict with one another.

Now let us get back to magic. Magic, according to Aleister Crowley, is a term that creates a striking distinction between performance magic such as what you'd see on a stage — pulling out rabbits from hats, sawing people in half — and the occult. The latter is more about mysticism and mysteries that cannot be described by scientists and cannot be neatly packaged as a religious fairy tale.

Crowley defines magic as "the Science and Art of causing Change to occur in conformity with Will," which involves the run-of-the-mill willful acts, and rituals. Basically, you can create the change you seek in any object, as long as that transformation is possible and allowed by the laws of nature.

The only way for you to understand your real self is for you to act in accordance with your true will. If you're going to make this happen, then you'll never find a better path or method than the practice of magic. In other words, it is vital that you come to accept the presence of magic within you. Your true will is the meeting point between your destiny and your free will.

In the words of Master Crowley, on page 134 of Magic, Book 4, *"One must find out for oneself, and make sure beyond doubt, who one is, what one is, why one is... Being thus conscious of the proper course to pursue, the next thing is to understand the conditions necessary to following it out. After that, one must eliminate from oneself every element alien or hostile to success, and develop those parts of oneself which are especially needed to control the aforesaid conditions."*

The Goal of Magic

You may wonder where the "k" in this spelling of magic comes from. No, it's not a typo; this is how it was spelled in Early Modern English, and this is the spelling you will find in all of Aleister Crowley's writings. Again, it distinguishes childish tricks and real power through knowledge and application of the occult.

With magic, you can create the change you seek by simply using the right kind of force, in the right amount, through the right method and appropriate mechanisms. It is a science because you've got to look at yourself under a figurative microscope so you can understand what makes you uniquely you. It's also an art because you've got to be able to take what you learn and apply it to your life in a way that yields results.

You can't divorce magic from the paranormal. Rather than let this frighten you, embrace it because the paranormal effects of magic will prove themselves useful to your development. Crowley himself testifies his own experiences with these powers, which appeared when he didn't really need them. He warned that they could be incredibly seductive and throw you off the path of discovering yourself. You do have to reject these powers or "Siddhi" as they are known in Ayurvedic philosophy.

Yet, Crowley admits there is still good to be had from these effects. Whenever you feel doubtful about the reality or potency, having these experiences will remind you that it's all very real and even the most advanced student must deal with these doubtful thoughts at times. So, the best way to use them is as a reminder that you are, indeed, on your true path.

A Rational Explanation of Magic

Unfortunately, there's a lot of misinformation about magic, especially since it is codified in metaphors and symbols which easily lend themselves to misinterpretation by the uninitiated or ignorant. So, what is magic really about? Well, keep your mind open, and prepare to be blown away.

Reconsidering Crowley's definition of magic, you'd think that magic means you can use supernatural powers to turn a pig into a unicorn or give a goat five extra legs. This is not the change that Crowley means by any stretch of the imagination. That's only possible in animation.

So, what is magic in the most rational and practical of definitions? Say you're thirsty. Your will is to quench your thirst. So, you go to the fridge, get yourself something to drink, and then you're no longer thirsty. You've created the change you sought in your body, or your physical reality, using your own will.

If magic were only about simple things such as quenching your thirst or feeding yourself, there'd be no point in reading this book or to the study of magic itself. You already know how to do those basic things. The example was simply to illustrate in the most basic way what magic is about. It is simply the process of actualizing the ideas you have in your mind by using your will to make them concrete. In other words, you use your will to manifest your desires into 3D reality.

Please realize that this doesn't mean everything you do is magical. For you to perform magic, you must possess the magician's mindset. You must understand innately that all the physicality is basically clay for you to mold into whatever form you will it to assume. Again, this has nothing to do with defying the preset laws of nature or physics. If anyone tells you they can fly off a building, I encourage you to cock your head at them and squint suspiciously while backing away ever so slowly. It simply understands that your life is yours to craft into whatever you want it to be. This is the magician's mindset. This is the position of true, pure power and limitlessness.

The key to having power in your life is to know who you are, what you are, and your reason for being. Once you have this knowledge, the next step on the path is to set a goal for yourself, preferably one you deeply resonate with. You must know exactly what it is you've got to do to produce these goals. The final step is to get rid of anything within you — within your mind — that would hinder making those goals a reality while honing the skills you'd need to make it all happen for you.

Say your goal is to become a world-renowned teacher on the laws of the universe. Well, you'd most definitely need to have some medium or platform to share your teachings with the world. That could mean conferences where you speak to crowds, or it could mean having a Twitter account where you drop 160 words of wisdom per tweet for people to follow along and digest.

However, you might have a weakness that would keep you away from achieving your goals. Say you're afraid of sharing your ideas, or you're deathly scared of having to speak to crowds. What do you do to eliminate this weakness? Well, you could gradually expose yourself to situations where you must speak with five, maybe ten people at a time.

You could also take classes on public speaking while you're at it, so you gain confidence and lose your fear of addressing the masses. You could attend karaoke, sing a song or two. You could recite poetry on open mic night. Whatever you do, you do it with the awareness that you're shaping your reality into one where you've achieved your set goal of teaching the world about how the universe works.

Magic and NLP

Let's talk about summoning demons — and try to get rid of preconceived notions about what demons are or aren't, for the time being. Assume that each day, you have a ritual that involves summoning a demon that allows you to speak with confidence and charisma, with no fear, no hesitation. This demon makes you feel invincible, strong, powerful.

Now, assume you're at a Ted Talk, and you're just about to start your presentation, so you summon this demon to assist you, so you don't fear the crowd, and you don't worry about whether you will fumble. This technique is not as outlandish as you think. It's simply Neuro-Linguistic Programming, which you may have heard of as NLP.

A very popular NLP technique is to assume that you're a giant. You're tall, strong, powerful, and you tower over everyone else in the room. When you imagine you're this powerful giant, you feel it in your body and in your mind. Now, when you have that feeling in you, you could press your thumb and middle finger to each other at the tips. That action is known as an anchor, meaning you're anchoring the feeling of being that invincible giant to the simple act of touching your middle finger and thumb together. Now, whenever you do that, the feeling automatically comes over you. You can use this anchor when you are about to give a speech, or you simply need a shot of courage and power. This works with the very same mechanism that happens when you hear a song, and your body and mind are instantly transported to the time and place when you first heard it.

The whole point of this is to make it clear to you that there's nothing crazy or unnatural about magic or rituals. It all has its roots in the human psyche. So if you ever assumed that you could make a portal appear in the sky using magic or that you could quite literally lift a mountain with your mind and cast it into the sea, then you should disabuse yourself of that notion right now. That last bit about casting a mountain into the sea was a popular parable in the Bible. A parable is a metaphor, a story that symbolizes an idea or a concept. To take it literally is foolishness. As a magic practitioner, you will continue to develop a sense of symbology and find true meaning where others lose their way.

The Power is Within You

People like Aleister Crowley understand that we all have within us the power to sculpt reality as we wish. We have the innate ability to take control of our lives and make of it what we will. This is echoed in the Thelemic principle that says, "Do what thou wilt." Sadly, many people have been deceived into thinking they must bow to an external God to achieve what they desire, without realizing that they themselves are God. That's right. You are God, master of your fate. Turn to no other than yourself to achieve your dreams.

The holy books are full of stories because it was the only way to explain psychology in terms that people could relate to. The wise men and women of those times turned to story and allegory to explain the mind's power, the power that lies within us all. Unfortunately, people have taken the allegorical and assumed that they're all literal.

This explains alchemy. It was never about the actual transformation of other materials into gold. It was simply a means to explain that to become the highest, grandest version of yourself, you will need to rid yourself of everything in you and about you that would stand in the path of you becoming golden. This means working on yourself psychologically.

Psychologist Jung knew of the true meaning of esoteric and gnostic teachings and made them a core part of his life's work. When you purify yourself by getting rid of your weaknesses and all tendencies that would stop you from achieving greatness, you transform yourself from unremarkable material to pure gold.

When Crowley spoke of understanding who you are, what you are, and why you are, he was referring to psychology. The more insight you have on yourself, the more you will increase in power. Your awareness will continue to grow and expand, which will lead to you having new, different, powerful ideas in your mind, which you can then use to shape your life as you desire.

The true magician is powerful because she has no doubt about who she is, what she is, and why she exists. She doesn't even call herself a magician. The word "magician" comes with a lot of baggage. Say to someone, "I'm a magician," and they will either assume you're nuts or ask for tickets to your next show, even if they have no intention of attending it. She is more about bringing her goals to pass in physical reality, understanding that the word "magic" is problematic.

In a Nutshell...

Magic is the art and science of manifesting using ritual, imagination, archetypes, and symbols. With ritual, you harness the energy needed to create your reality, to influence things to go your way.

There are those who assume that it is a thing of madness. "It's all in your head," they tell you. It's all made up. Yet, it is hard to dismiss the effect that magical rituals have on your body. You feel the crackling energy, and you sense the changes in your way of thinking. You see actual changes in the way you live your life and actual results. For something that's all in your head, the magic of ritual is undeniably powerful. You can easily say to the nonbelievers, as Lon Milo DuQuette wrote, "It's all in your head... You just have no idea how big your head is."

Some people look at magic through the lens of energy. They believe that the practitioner of magic simply generates energy that interacts with matter so it creates change, whether near or far. Neuroscientists argue this energy is self-generated, arising from your brain and nervous system. Others, including quantum physicians, say that consciousness or energy is what the universe is made of itself; and the latter is proving more and more to be the case. Read Dr. Dean Radin's "Real Magic" for more on the subject of thought-influencing matter.

When it comes to magic, the last mindset assumes that it all happens by asking for the help of spirits or angels to make our goals come to pass. To accept this would mean we must also accept there is a whole other spectrum of life to which we're not privy as humans, a whole other universe we can interact with by deliberately being aware of it. Whether these beings do exist, simply acting on the assumption that they're real and will help you do produce remarkable results each time.

If you recall nothing else about magic, then keep these three things in mind:

- **Magic is About Intention.** You know what you *really* want, not what you only think you want. This is your intention, unconditioned and untamed by doubts or beliefs about being unworthy or not deserving of your intention. You will know your objective by how much joy it gives you and how much it effuses your whole being with light and enthusiasm.

- **Magic is About Attention.** You must focus on your purpose with an unwavering mind and heart. The more you can feel it, imagine it, and accept it, the faster you allow the intention to unfold and crystalize into 3D reality.

- **Magic is About Action.** You cannot just sit at home, visualize a bag of money in your closet, or a lover in your bed, and then just wait home for those things to come to you. There is action involved. You act as a show of faith that your goal has come to pass, and you put yourself in a position where you're ready to receive your goal. Things do work out on their own after your ritual, but you should do the things you have to do to be ready to receive the physical manifestation of your blessing.

Chapter Two: Magical Law: Do What You Will

What comes to your mind when you read the magical law, "Do what thou wilt?" The license to do whatever you please, whenever, no matter the consequences? Well, that's not what Crowley meant by that. Sadly, this phrase is often misunderstood, even by those who claim to be in the know when it comes to occult matters. "Do what you will" doesn't mean you should engage in debauchery or overindulgence. Crowley's original philosophy wasn't losing yourself to whatever whims come upon you. His quote was referring to True Will.

Discovering Your True Will: The Key to Transformation

To learn your True Will, you must find your True Self. When you learn this, then you must do just that. You must "do what you will." It's not about giving yourself carte blanche to go on a killing spree or sacrifice the young and innocent. Do what you will by discovering your life's true purpose, finding your diving path, and staying on that path, ignoring all else.

Crowley, ever-prolific, gave various definitions during his life. True Will is essentially your energy. It is that which you are to spend your lifetime or lifetimes expressing. Crowley puts it beautifully when he says, "True Will is the reason for your incarnation". According to Crowley in Magic Without Tears, to discover yours, "You must find an answer to the question: 'How did I come to be in this place at this time, engaged in this particular work?"

The essence of "do what thou wilt" is simply this: The only right you have is to do your True Will at all times – in thought, word, and deed. To be clear, at no point will your Truth ever cause others pain or despair. It will never rob other stars like you of their own rights to follow their own truth. This principle does not give you permission to hurt others willfully, take advantage of them, or put them in a dangerous position.

Find your True Will. When you do, remember that it will not involve cheating others or being dishonest. Nor will it involve tricking people into doing things they wouldn't ordinarily do of their own free will against their best interests, manipulating them, or any of that ugliness.

Crowley likened it to the Tao. Most people assume that it is all about action, but it's about much more than that. It is energy you manifest in whatever form you will. Think about the Tao for a moment. For following the Tao, there's no conscious thought. It's all energy flowing along naturally, much like a river flows downstream, unaided and unimpeded. It all moves along with the force of authenticity. The river isn't thinking to itself, "I'm headed to the sea." The river isn't being guided by anything other than the natural position of the rocks and the riverbed around it. It moves with its authentic, natural laws as coded in nature. It moves with the Tao.

In Magic Without Tears, chapter XXXIV, Crowley likens it to a planet moving in harmony with other planets while on its own path. When another planetary body comes too close, the planet makes a little adjustment with no force, no disagreement, all so it can continue in its own orbit. This suggests what we covered in chapter one, that everyone is a star in their own right, with their own to discover and pursue. When you have found yours, it will not impinge on another's ability to follow their Truth. Every star remains in a state of balance with every other star. In being your authentic self, you will create balance in your life, and this balance will ripple out to the universe, creating the lasting change you seek in your reality.

The Inscription on the Door to the Mystical: Man, Know Thyself

You must identify yourself to access the divine mysteries of the universe and harness them for your good and the good of others. To know yourself, you must be yourself and observe who that self really is. But how can you be yourself in a world that continues to insist you shouldn't color outside the lines? How do you become authentic in a world that says from one side of its mouth, "Be unapologetically you," and on the other side it says, "Okay, reign it back in. That's too much 'you' going on." Dare to explore yourself outside of what society and media say is okay, and you're crucified for it.

It's so hard to be who you are since it means you must deal with disagreements with family, friends, and the world in general. It almost seems pointless. Why deliberately start a fight with the whole world on one side and you standing alone?

Here's why it's worth it for you to know yourself: It's the only way you will ever find pure, lasting happiness. If you do not know yourself, your real Self, then you cannot find your True Will; and if you cannot find it, let alone act on it, then you will be condemned to a life brimming with sadness and dissatisfaction. Crowley writes in Magic in Theory and Practice that each one of us is "unsatisfactory to himself until he has established himself in his right relation with the Universe." This right relation is your True Will, born of self-knowledge.

Listen, if you're doing anything outside of your this, then it is a waste of time and effort. Those who go against it, ignorantly or by choice, will find that their hopes and dreams are like a river attempting to go from moving downstream to flowing upstream: An impossibility.

You must know yourself, so you can let go of hanging branches and treacherously smooth stones, and simply allow yourself to be carried downstream to your desire, which is ever present, and just waiting for you to stop fighting it.

Going downstream doesn't mean your path will be easy or there will not be stumbling blocks along your way. You'll have to deal with these things; that's the nature of life. You'll deal with pushback in the form of family, friends, and society, who will not be able to understand your purpose. They mean well, but often, yours runs contrary to the plans they have for you, and so they will fight it. You can be sure of that. Still, the reward of staying true to your authentic self is *very much* worth it.

Do all you can to make a lion bark and a frog meow. No matter what, you will never succeed. But allow each animal their natural sound, and you have discovered the secret to moving ahead in life. You can learn that the inertia of the Universe can carry you much further along your path than you can by trying to muscle your path into make something work out that was never for you in the first place!

Dispelling the Myths Surrounding the Magical Law

Again, there are too many misconceptions surrounding the *magical law..* To help you stay the course and make progress with magic, you must know the truth. So, let's rid ourselves of these lies and misunderstandings.

Myth #1: You Only Find Your True Will at a Particular Point in Time. For some reason, there's a myth going around that there's a certain moment that you get to discover what your true will is. This myth suggests that while you may not know your will, at some point in the future, it will come upon you in an experience or a flash of insight.

The truth is as penned by Crowley in <u>Liber II: Message of the Master Therion</u>: "The will is but the dynamic aspect of the self..."

In other words, it is just you expressing yourself naturally. Your true nature will be expressed, whether in full or diluted, with preconceived notions about who you should be. So, we're always engaging in it. If we are, what then is the purpose of all this "find your True Will" talk? It's simple: The point being made is that we could do a better job of doing what we want, by being more aware of what we want and doing so with more commitment and intention. Sudden insights do happen, but that event doesn't change that your Truth is moment-by-moment, dynamic, and worth pursuing at all costs.

Myth #2: True Will Can Only be Found in the Distant Future. Much like the previous myth, people think to themselves, "I may not have a clue what my Will is right now, but I'll know it when I see it... in the future... hopefully." This is not an unreasonable thought, but again, the magician should remember that every day, every moment, we're acting on our will to some degree. Perhaps, rather than saying ""Find your True Will," we might say "Become more aware of your True Self and seek to understand it better."

When you think of it as a thing to be discovered, it makes you less eager to do or be what you are at the moment. It makes you defer things to a later date. You look around you as you live the crummy life you don't want and say, "If only I knew what my *True Will* is!" when it would be even more beneficial to consider the present circumstances and see what can be done in the now.

Myth #3: Either You're Acting on Your True Will – or You're Not. Will is not a black and white thing. There are many shades of gray. It all comes down to how much you pursue it. Remember this, and you'll find the journey much easier since you won't be bogged down by doubt or guilt about whether you're staying true to yourself. You know that you're following your path, and the only adjustment you need to make is to be more engaged and intentional about remaining faithful to your path 100 percent.

Myth #4: True Will is Only One Thing, and it Never Changes. This is far from the truth. Will has nothing to do with "the perfect job" or anything like that. It is a combination of your various talents, hobbies and proclivities, dreams, and aspirations. It will involve so much more than just wearing one hat as "teacher," or "doctor," or "mother."

You cannot isolate a single thing and say, "It is my will to be a parent." Well, if all you are is a parent, what are you when you *go to work*? Are you a parent at your legal firm? Well, obviously not; you're a lawyer. When you get back home, do you play attorney to your kids and family? These questions may seem silly, but they serve to illustrate that it isn't just tied to one thing; it's very dynamic, changing from moment to moment.

Myth #5: True Will Can be Summed Up in a Phrase. I hope you see why this one's a myth. If it is dynamic (and it is), then how do you sum it up in a neat phrase? Now, it is beneficial to try to do that, so you have an expression by which to judge whether you're following your Truth *at the moment.* Say a phrase goes, "It is my Will to have the fullness of health," which would mean you have no business eating that third pack of candy bars.

Well, then, what other phrases would you have to define your character when confronted with a situation that tempts you to cheat? And what other phrase would you have when faced in a place where you question the abundance of the universe and its availability to you? You cannot sum it up in a phrase because it is beyond words. Crowley put it this way: *"Also reason is a lie; for there is a factor infinite and unknown; all their words are skew-wise."* You can find this quote in Liber AL vel Legis, II:32.

Myth #6: Finding Your True Will Means Having a Mystical Experience. You do not need a highly evolved being to appear and tell you what it is. You need not have ayahuasca before you know. You don't need to "attain enlightenment." Sure, these experiences might lend you clarity and help keep your ego in check, but remember that Will is always present, and it's constantly acted upon to a degree, and it can be more intentionally expressed.

You don't need a special mystical background to know that a certain relationship or friendship is no longer in harmony with you. You don't need a mystical experience to let you know that time to switch career paths or time to follow your dreams actively. Do not mistakenly assume that your lack of a magical understanding gives you a free hall pass to avoid your Will.

Myth #7: Your True Will is True for Everyone Else. There is no such thing as the "ideal magician." There's no gold standard by which one can measure all Thelemites. It is not your place to decide for others what is right or wrong for them or what their True Will is. In The Vision, it is written, "The man of the earth is adherent. The lover giveth his life unto the work among men. The hermit goeth solitary and giveth only of his light unto men."

Put another way: Some people are of the earth, others are hermits, and a few are lovers. It is different for us all. One might seek spiritual illumination, and another may seek to live a life free of such concerns. None of these are wrong, and to insist that your path is the one true path is not only very egotistical, but it also hints of a holier-than-thou attitude, and is the complete antithesis of full liberty, which is the hallmark of the Law.

Myth #8: Your Will Has No Connection with Others Around You. While we're all individual stars, we're all interconnected in the same galaxy. We're affected by the world around us, and in turn, we affect the world as well. In other words, your actions are not contained in a bubble; they ripple out into the universe.

If it is your will to eat only meat, then animals are affected. If it is your will to eat only plants, plants are affected. If it is to be generous, well, you can be charitable only to others. To attain enlightenment, that means your environment and circumstances must be affected in some way to allow you that experience.

With this in mind, if you notice you keep facing a lot of difficulties when you do certain things, you might want to think of it as a message saying you need to change what you're doing or how you're doing it, rather than being so stubborn and insisting "My way or the highway."

Myth #9: True Will Exempts You From Suffering. Again, finding and following it to the best of your abilities does not mean you will not face adversity. Suffering is a part of life. We fall ill; we lose people, we forget stuff, we die. That's just life. Just because you're experiencing something doesn't mean you're automatically a failure at staying true to your will. Suffering allows you to grow, learn, and become more than you ever were.

As a true Thelemite, you're not interested in transcending the physical material world. You're not looking to avoid pain and suffering. Acknowledging suffering as part of life sets you free from the bondage of unnecessary feelings. There lies the distinction. A lot of misery is not the natural kind, nor is it needed. Instead, it is born of the undisciplined mind, fed by lies and misconceptions both from within and without. It is this *unnecessary* suffering that it exempts you from.

Myth #10: True Will Exempts You From Conflict. Like suffering, differences cannot be avoided in life. There will always be those who do not see things how you do. Even as you do this practice (and they do theirs), they will not always see eye-to-eye with you. There's nothing inherently wrong with a disagreement. The trouble is in how the difference is *perceived.*

When doing this and allowing others the right to follow theirs, you come to understand that it's okay to perceive things differently. You let go of the impulse to insist that your approach is the right way or the only way —a mindset that causes a lot of disagreements to devolve into terrible outcomes like betrayal, war, and oppression.

It doesn't mean conflicts end. You just come to an understanding you have no right to place your standards and expectations on anyone else, just as they have no right to impinge on your chosen manner of self-expression or beliefs. This is why it says in AL III:42, "...argue not, convert not, talk not overmuch!"

With these myths debunked, it should be even clearer in your mind right now and should help you grow in awareness in every moment.

Chapter Three: Meditation: The Power of the Mind

That you're reading this right now says that you know just how vital it is for you to find your True Will. It says you're willing to explore it, to pursue it, and allow yourself to express it more each day. For that, commend yourself.

True Will does not readily make itself obvious, particularly to those who haven't spent time looking for it. If only it were as simple as figuring out your career, then you could at least have somewhere to start your search! You now know that True Will is about so much more than that. It is your very reason for being, for breathing.

As an initiate of magic, it is your duty to not only discover your True Will but to act it out to the best of your abilities, from one moment to the next. This is the purpose of real magic. Everything else is simply fluff and feathers. It seems so simple, and it is, theoretically. With actual practice, it can be rather difficult.

You already know that how to realize all you want in life is to follow your bliss, allow your heart or joy to guide you to what matters the most to you. But such sentiments never make it clear that these things are not simply a given. Becoming the grandest and best version of yourself doesn't simply happen. It's never been that way. It never will be. There is an element of work.

To assume these desirable traits just fall into one's lap is the same as assuming that all you need to do to build muscles is to just sit and do nothing. You've got to train. You've got to break down muscle to allow it to repair itself so that you become stronger and develop even more muscle and strength. You'll also need guidance so that you do not train in a way that makes your efforts futile, at best – or puts you in danger, at worst.

The same principle of working out your body to build muscles applies to discovering your True Will and exercising it. You will need to train and pay attention to who you're now being, so you can adjust accordingly until you align with the person you'd like to become, which is the greatness you know you are. To achieve this greatness, you will need practice. You'll need tools and you'll need various techniques and methods to train yourself. The methods and tools you need the most are meditation and magic. It is to the former we will give our attention in this chapter.

Meditation: The Skeleton Key to the Magical

There is no method to help you connect with the magical within you that works better than meditation. This is as old as time itself. It is very precise, and it always yields results without fail if you use methods that are authentic and not the run-of-the-mill garbage peddled by charlatans who would have you believe that they have the key to your salvation.

Meditation works... when you work it. You will need to remember the two stages of work as you begin your journey.

- The journey within yourself to discover your True Will.
- The application of your body, mind, and soul towards the manifestation of your True Will.

Do not let that it is work scare you away from doing what you must. It is the only work that will reward you exceedingly, far above and beyond anything else you might think of.

No one is born knowing precisely what path their life should take. If that were the case, then we'd have no struggle. We'd simply be off and running, going about the business of fulfilling our destiny. That is NOT how this works.

When you're born, you're born tabula rasa — other than your innate True Will, that is. Over time, you find you get a lot of impressions about what you should and shouldn't do, or be, or have. However, your True Will remains within you, waiting to be discovered or to be expressed even more than you allow it to be. It waits for you to become mindful of your very own divine authority over your life. You become more aware of your authority through the constant practice of meditation.

With meditation, you find that the veil that covers all eyes and makes all believe that they are simply bound to experience life happening to them falls off. You become more aware of the power within you. You learn just how powerful you are. It hits you that you have a magic wand within you — free will — which you can use to craft the life you prefer.

Meditation: The Art of Mindfulness

A very critical part of Buddhist practice is *sati*, which is awareness, or mindfulness. Mindfulness involves becoming very much conscious of the here and now. Most people's minds are either stuck in the past in regret or reminiscence or stuck in the future in worry or anticipation. Sadly, it is a rare person who is fully present in the here and now. The practice of meditation teaches you to become more aware, more present, here and now. In being tethered and grounded in the present, you're better able to decipher what your True Will dictates to you at the moment.

There are several meanings of the Buddhist word *sati*, besides mindfulness. Sati is derived from the Pali word sati and the Sanskrit smrti. Originally, smrti meant "to recollect" or "to remember" or "to bear in mind." These meanings were in connection to the Vedic tradition of memorizing sacred scripture.

According to the Satipatthana Sutta, sati means "to maintain one's awareness of reality." It further defines mindfulness (sati) as being aware that what you perceive with your senses is nothing more than illusions. This awareness allows you to see the true nature of life around you. Inevitably, the more you practice meditation, the more mindful you become, and the clearer your True Will becomes in your mind.

Meditation Techniques

Technique #1: Altered Consciousness. Find a comfortable place to sit in loose, comfy clothes, and shut your eyes. You may light incense or a candle or play some relaxing, calming music before you begin, but none of that is necessary. Such things may be a hindrance because, ideally, you want to hit a point where you can practice wherever you are, whether there are candles, music, incense, or not. These things only help you initially.

Now notice the top of your head. As you do, start to scan your body by directing that awareness from your head, slowly working your way down to your feet. As you become aware of each part of your body, allow it to relax. Notice the parts where you feel the most stress or resistance. When you feel areas on your body with tension, imagine that relaxing waves of warm light flow from the top of your head, and through these parts, clearing out all tension and unease. Do your best to relax.

Breathe in, deep as you can, making sure your lungs are filled all the way. Through your slightly parted lips, let the air go. You want each inhales and exhale to feel even deeper than the last one. Imagine your breath is like a gentle wind that blows back and forth, a never-ending, relaxing cycle. All troublesome thoughts are only clouds, which the gentle winds of your breath blow away into nothingness. Your job is not to control your thoughts. Simply allow them to pass, blown away by the wind.

Move your attention to your heart and feel the energy as it beats and moves blood around your body. Feel the love within, your love for all the people you hold dear. Feel the light in your heart. There's no need to actually see anything. Know it's there and accept it. Finally, feel the divine spark within your soul. Know that in your soul is a flame, whose light continues to burn bright and guide you along your way.

This exercise puts you in touch with the four elements of magic: By putting your body at ease, you've worked with the earth element. By sweeping away all throughs from your mind and focusing on your breath, you've worked with the air element. Focusing on your heart, love, and blood is the water element, and your soul connects you with the fire element.

Slowly countdown from ten to one as you breathe, imagining that you're writing each number on a board and then erasing it. This way, your conscious mind is ready to handle whatever task you give it. When you get to one, begin the countdown again, this time with just your inner voice, so your intuition becomes active. When you're done, you will be in an altered state. Enjoy it. This is the state of meditation, from which you can work your magic for the good of all. When you're ready to come back out of it, simply count up from one to ten, then breathe regularly, and really feel your body. Have a good stretch. If you feel out of touch, place your hands on the floor and push them in, or you can lie on your back on the floor and feel connected to it.

Technique #2: Standing Meditation. You'll want to make sure you're barefoot for this. Find somewhere quiet, shut your eyes, and keep your shoulders relaxed. Move your awareness to your feet. Feel what your feet on the floor. Pay attention to what you notice about how you're feeling. Is the middle of your feet making less contact with the ground than your heels and toes? Is the pressure even or different in spots? What about the temperature? Do you feel very little, if anything? Then try moving your feet around or rocking back and forth on them so you can feel various sensations. Notice as many of them as you can.

Technique #3: Listening Meditation. Find a place where you can hear all sorts of sounds; a restaurant, the park, a lake, or wherever. You can also do this technique while you wait at the airport or while you wait in a queue. There's no need to keep your eyes shut, though it could be incredibly helpful for some people to do that.

Now, pay attention to every sound around you. Do your best to tell them apart and notice how they contrast with one another. There are sounds that are louder, others softer. They may be deeper, and others may be shrill. Some are close, while others further off. Some are nice, while others are irritating. Notice them all. Then focus on one sound for some time before moving your attention to the next.

Technique #4: Walking Meditation. You'll want to keep your shoes and socks off for this one, too. You also want to keep your eyes open, so you don't walk into something. Whether you're with others or alone, you can do this meditation, as long as you're not disturbed. You can do this in your room, simply walking back and forth, taking your time with each step (but not as slow as, say, the sloths from that cartoon). As you move, notice your feet as they hit the ground and rise again. You can also notice all the sensations you feel in your legs, thighs, knees, calves, and angles. Just follow all the sensations you can.

Technique #5: Looking Meditation. Ideally, do this outside. If you can't get outside, then a large enough room can work just fine. You want to look at something that's close to you, perhaps a flower or your coffee mug. Look closely at every detail you find, from the varying shades to the patterns, colors, and shapes of whatever has your attention. Spend a minute or two looking at this object, then move to an object further off in the distance. Look at it with the same degree of attention for a minute or two. When you're finished, return your attention to the first object you studied, and see if you spot things you hadn't seen the first time.

Why Meditate?

As you practice these exercises, you will notice that you're much better at clearing your mind and silencing your thoughts to cut right through to the truth of any matter at the moment. You'll be more cognizant of where your thoughts are most of the time, and as such, you will be able to halt any thoughts that do not resonate with your True Will before they have the chance to gain enough traction to make a mess of things.

Meditation does a lot more than help you become aware of the moment. It helps you train your mind so it only ever does your bidding. It cannot be run on your behalf by any subliminal messages in the media or any dark, depressing stuff from the dreary world around you.

With meditation, you can tell whether you're feeding your soul with faith and the good things of life or whether you're stuffing it full of fear. You need to make sure your mind is focused on the right things. The mind does not discriminate, and it will bring you exactly what you focus on. With meditation, you're more aware of where you put your attention. Your attention is gold. Don't squander it. The best way to be sure you're not wasting it all is to make meditation a daily practice.

Chapter Four: Yoga: The Magic of the Physical Body

There are two very critical elements in terms of spiritual attainment, according to the law of Thelema. One is magic. The other is Yoga.

Self-Discovery and Self Realization through Yoga

Yoga, by its very nature, is all a process through which you discover yourself. It's not a religion, as people erroneously believe, and there's no evil in it either. It's all a practice through which you learn about who you really are and what you bring to the cosmic table, so to speak. As you go through the process of Yoga, you clear your mind of all cobwebs so you can see yourself, others, and the world around you in their truest forms.

You cannot be separate from your identity. So discovering yourself and realizing who you are is not something as basic as taking off an outfit and putting on another. Changing your character is also different from simply cramming all the verses and dogma of a religion or whatever into your mind, as most religions are guilty of doing.

Yoga is a very personal journey in which you must come to know yourself intimately. You discover your genuine nature by having your own experiences and perceiving things from your own perspective. So, think of Yoga as a science rather than a religion you can sign up for today only to renounce tomorrow. There's an entire process to it. The truly self-realized are those who have undergone the process of Yoga, which is the revelation of everything in its true form.

Here lies the key distinction between Yoga and religion: You may join a religion and not necessarily practice it to be considered part of that church, but with Yoga, you join nothing; you practice.

Many people erroneously assume that Yoga is akin to a religious sect, or a cult, or a team you join so you have the satisfaction of being a part of something bigger than you. Yoga is a set of values, tools, and virtues – all of which make up a process that leads you to become your best self physically, spiritually, and mentally. This is where many people give up on Yoga because they cannot "join" it; they can only practice it, and practice requires discipline.

Yoga is not about blind belief, but growing in wisdom and love for others. It's a solitary process, and so you must find your strength within you, and not from outside you in the form of a group. You can't join Yoga, which means *you can't quit it either.* It is your duty to yourself to continue to discover that part of you that is greater than the costume of flesh and blood you've got on right now.

A Brief History of Yoga

Yoga's history is so full of uncertainty because its sacred texts were passed on from one generation to the next by oral tradition. Plus, the instructions were mostly secretive. The earliest records of Yoga teachings were etched on palm leaves, too fragile and easy to destroy, get damaged, or be lost. While Yoga is said to have advanced over the course of 5,000 years, there are those who believe it's twice as old as that.

Four distinct periods matter the most when it comes to development, practice, and innovations in Yoga.

Pre-Classical Yoga: Yoga was initially developed over 5,000 years ago in Northern India by a civilization known as the Indus-Sarasvati. The word Yoga itself was first written in the Rig Veda, one of the oldest and most sacred texts made up of mantras, songs, and rituals used by Vedic priests called Brahmans.

The Brahmans helped to develop Yoga, slowly, along with mystic seers called Rishis. They all took time to document their beliefs, and their practices in what is called the *Upanishads* — which has over 200 scriptures, including the renowned Bhagavad-Gita, penned sometime around 500 B.C.E. What the Upanishads did was to reframe the ritual sacrifice covered in the Vedas and make it an internal process, one which involves sacrificing the ego on the altar of wisdom (jnana yoga), self-knowledge, and action (karma yoga).

Classical Yoga: Where the pre-classical stage was full of contradictory yogic ideas, the classical period had a more systematic and organized approach to the principals, because of Patanjali's Yoga-Sutras, which were written during the second century. This text goes over the ideal path of Raja Yoga, which is usually called "classical yoga." Patanjali brought order to Yoga by creating its eight-limbed path, which detailed the necessary steps and stages of the process required to gain enlightenment or Samadhi. Until now, Patanjali's Yoga-Sutras continue to influence several styles of Yoga as we know it today.

Post-Classical Yoga: Centuries after the reform Patanjali brought about, a collection of Yogis came together to form a system or series of practices that give long life and revive the body. As one, they spurned all ancient Vedic teachings and focused on using the physical body to achieve Samadhi. These Yogis created Tantra Yoga, which had techniques designed to clean both mind and body to shed off everything that tethered us to the physical world. This is how Hatha Yoga came to be.

Modern Yoga: From the late 1800s to early 1900s, there was an exodus of Yoga masters from the East to the West. These masters attracted a following, notably from the Parliament of Religions in 1893, in Chicago, when a particular Master — Swami Vivekananda — blew away his attendees with his amazing insights on Yoga. By the 1920s and 1930s, India was heavily into Hatha Yoga, thanks to Swami Sivananda, T. Krishnamacharya, and other well-known Hatha Yoga practitioners. The first Hatha Yoga school was founded in 1924 by Krishnamacharya. Then there was the Divine Life Society, right on the Ganges River banks, established by Sivananda in 1936.

Three students — T.K.V. Desikachar, B.K.S. Iyengar and Pattabhi Jois — having been tutored by Krishnamacharya, made sure his legacy continued and that Hatha Yoga became more popular than ever. Sivananda had penned over 200 books about Yoga, set up nine ashrams, and an impressive number of yoga centers globally.

Yoga made its way to the West in little bits, until 1947, when Indra Devi set up her Hollywood Yoga studio. Ever since that happened, there have been a lot more Indian and Western Yoga teachers sharing their knowledge of Hatha Yoga and garnering followers in the millions. Now, there are all sorts of Hatha Yoga styles, which focus on various aspects of this sacred practice.

Mystical Uses of Yoga in the Past

Shamanic practices and Sadhana Yoga come together to create the magic of mystical yoga, in which your inner mystic is brought to light. The whole point of this style is to reveal your true essence, the whole point of your existence, or if you prefer, your True Will.

There are three very distinct levels which the mystical Yoga practitioner needed to remember back then. These levels remain relevant even in today's times. First, you must know the foundation of it all. This foundation comprises a routine of vital postures connected with sequences and transitional breath. Next, you must know the modification level. In other words, the practitioner would have to learn to modify the original sequences and postures to match her ability and understanding. The final level involves integration. Mystical Yoga has always been based on the mystic's personal experience as they journey to the very essence of themselves. With the integration, the mystic can better personalize the routines they've learned, giving more meaning to each.

There are so many routines involved in Mystical Yoga, from Shamanic Yoga, Hatha Flow Yoga, Restorative Yoga, and Gentle Yoga, to Mystical Vinyasa Yoga. No matter the routine, Mystical Yoga has always been a spiritual practice that follows this sequence, typically:

1. The names of deities and/or spirits and connecting energies are chanted to allow the mystic Yogi or Yogini to connect with their higher self.

2. Intentions are set once the Yogi becomes aware of his inner being so the practice deepens, and it operates on all levels, obvious and subtle.

3. Breathing exercises are done to create a deeper meditative state.

4. The practitioner warms up with easy, gentle stretches, performed while kneeling, seated, and standing. They also perform sun salutations.

5. Standing and sitting sequences are initiated.

6. The practitioner performs a series of postures in a closing sequence that works on each chakra in the body.

7. Then the practitioner goes into relaxation, using progressive relaxation of each muscle group and autosuggestion to release all blocked energy in the body, bringing the mind into a clear state with no thought, just a simple awareness of the nothingness of the universe.

8. The Yogini connects with her intention by meditating about spiritual concepts.

9. Finally, the practitioner chants the deity or spirit's name from before in appreciation, certain that her intention has been fulfilled.

Yoga According to Aleister Crowley

Crowley has written two books on Yoga and the appropriate breathing techniques. His <u>Magic: Liber ABA</u> (Book IV) and <u>Eight Lectures on Yoga</u> give the Magus (a practitioner of Magic) a lot of detail to learn meditation and Yogic breathing.

First Practice

For your first practice, Crowley suggests that you focus on breathing and nothing else. Tell yourself repeatedly, "The breath flows in," as you inhale, and as you exhale, say to yourself, "The breath flows out."

As you do this, you want to ensure you track your results. How long did you practice? You want to make sure you practiced for at least 20 minutes. Note how you did with concentration. Note how often you broke focus and notice what kind of distractions took you away from your breath. Notice your emotional, physical, and mental states as you focused on your breath. Write down the date and time and how you felt or perceived yourself and the world around you after you were done.

Crowley says that when you do this diligently, you may very well experience Samadhi or enlightenment, which is the final limb of Patanjali's Yoga-Sutras' eight limbs.

Second Practice

Here's a second practice, as explained in <u>Liber RV</u>, involving pranayama. Pranayama comprises the Sanskrit words prana, meaning "life," and *ayama,* which means "extend" or "draw out." Pranayama is about controlling your breath, which clears out your subtle energy channels (*nadis*) all over your body, and awakens the Kundalini (or *serpent power*) that sits at the bottom of your spine.

The kind of breathing you'll do in this practice is known as *Nadi Suddhi pranayama, r Anuloma pranayama, or Nadi Shodhana pranayama,* or in English, alternate nostril breathing.

Steps for Alternate Nostril Breathing

1. Take a seat in an asana. With your left thumb, close your right nostril. Breath out as slow as you can through your left nostril, for up to 20 seconds. Then breathe in through that same nostril for 10 seconds.

2. Next, switch thumbs, and close your left nostril this time. Breathe in through your right nostril for up to 20 seconds, and then for 10 seconds.

3. Continue to alternate your hands and do this for an hour. If you're only starting, begin with 20 minutes, and work your way up with each new session.

4. Eventually, you should exhale for 30 seconds and inhale for 15 seconds.

5. When it's easy for you to breathe for the times mentioned in the previous step (and not a moment before, warns Crowley), exhale for 15 seconds, inhale for 15 seconds, and then hold your breath for 15 seconds. Continue with this until you can do this easily for an hour.

6. Now, increase your exhale time to 40 seconds and your inhale time to 20 seconds.

7. Once this time is easy for you; exhale for 20 seconds, inhale for 10 seconds, and hold your breath for 30 seconds.

8. Doing step 7 comfortably means you're ready for harder techniques. Crowley writes that you should become proficient at a cycle with a ratio of 10:20:40 seconds, or 16:32:64, and longer. It is vital that you build up to those lengths gradually.

Crowley warns that if there's food in your stomach, it will make your practice harder, no matter how little there is. So, you want to be mindful of eating before your pranayama practice.

He adds that you must not strain yourself because you do not want to go so out of breath you breathe too fast or you gasp for air. It is important you keep your breathing full, deep, and regular. You'll need a journal to note down all the magical things you experience as you practice, as well as to analyze your results.

When you perform pranayama the right way, your body will be covered in perspiration, much different from the kind you get from heat or a workout. You can rub this sweat back into your body to gain strength. Your body will also go rigid, automatically. You will then have spasmodic movements of your body, which you're aware of even in your unconsciousness. It can seem like there's no weight to you, and an unseen force moves you. Also, your body will levitate and remain suspended for anywhere from one second to over an hour.

Third Practice

Consider this to be a walking variation of the previous pranayama practice. It's known as Bhraman pranayama or "walking breath."

Steps for Walking Breath

1. As you walk, breathe in and out, deeply and fully.

2. Chant a mantra in a rhythm that matches each footstep. You could chant *Om; Om mani padme hum;* or *Om Shanti, Shanti, Shanti.*

3. You'll begin the pranayama but using both nostrils and without holding your breath. Rather than breathing for specific counts, you'll breathe in tandem with your steps. You could breathe in for four steps and then breathe out for four.

4. Up the number of steps per inhale and exhale to 6 each, then 8 each, then 12, then 16, and then 24 or more if you can.

5. Next, switch it up by inhaling for 6 steps and exhaling for 12. Then you can go from 6:12 to 8:16, and move on to 12:24 or even more if you can.

6. Finally, add in the Kumbhakam, which is holding your breath. Start by inhaling for 4 steps, holding for 4 steps, then exhaling for 4 steps. Then you can move on to 2 steps per inhale, 8 steps per hold, 4 steps per exhale, and 8 steps per hold. You can up the count in a ratio of 1:4:2.

Fourth Practice

1. Begin the walking pranayama from the third practice. Find your rhythm with your steps, breathing, and mantra.

2. Go faster and faster with your steps and your mantra until your walking becomes a dance.

Crowley advocates using the basic waltz rhythm for your steps (left-right-left, right-left-right, and so on). Your mantra must be in three-time. If it is dedicated to a deity, you could turn this meditation into a form of worship. However, Crowley says it's better to use a mantra that paints an abstract idea of the supreme God.

Fifth Practice

1. Begin with your walking pranayama and get into a nice rhythm with your mantra, steps, and breathing. Allow it all to become a dance.

2. Now, allow the dance to be free of your will. You do this by zoning out into a state of trance, allowing your spirit to flow through your dancing body. This is not a conscious thing. You will know when you've achieved this state. You may occasionally exercise your will, but with practice, learn to let it go.

The same phenomena as described for the second practice of alternate nostril breathing may happen again with this.

Sixth Practice

This practice involves breathing fast and shallow. It can also include meditation on your Vishuddha chakra while you chant its mantra "ham." This chakra is your throat chakra, which oversees self-expression and communication. It acts as a purifier. Through this chakra, amrita or "the elixir of life" flows down. This elixir can either be poisonous, or it can lead to immortality. With this open, you allow yourself to receive wisdom in abundance. When it's closed, decay and death follow.

1. Breathe. Make it as rapidly and shallowly as you can.

2. Get into a position you'd be in if you'd just exhaled with force. Drop your chin slightly, tucking it close to your chest while pushing your tongue against your palate.

3. You must breathe using only your throat muscles.

4. If you wish, you can increase the period between each breath.

5. As you do this, keep your attention on your Vishuddha chakra.

Seventh Practice

This one is to the point. You must breathe as rapidly and deeply as you can. It's almost the same thing as the Ujjayi breathing technique, or "the ocean breath," often used in Taoist and Hindu Yoga practices. You inhale as deeply as you can, making sure your lower belly is full, then your rib cage rises, and your upper chest and throat. It's hard to pull this off *too fast*.

This practice is almost like the Breath of Fire, a technique by Yogi Bhajan, a teacher of Kundalini Yoga. You need to breathe as fast as you can, pumping our breath using the power of your belly, in and out. When your lungs fill with air, force it all out right away. The moment your lungs are empty, force the air back in. Soon, the rhythm will become an automatic thing. Use enough force, but don't contract your diaphragm.

Mens Sana in Corpore Sano

Mens sana in corpore sano is a Latin phrase that simply means "a healthy mind in a healthy body." As a practitioner of magic, you must guard your health zealously. This is because your body and mind are tools you use to discover and express your Will.

You are not your body, and you are not your mind either. However, your state of consciousness is often what determines your physical condition. In other words, you must be aware of what thoughts go about in your mind because those images affect your body's health. The Magus must always guard his energy, making sure to meditate and to continually seek ways to stay in touch with the divine. As you practice Yoga and meditation daily, you keep your mind and body in an optimum state that allows you to fulfill your highest goal: Your True Will.

Chapter Five: Magical Astral Travel Techniques

There is so much more to the world than what you can presently perceive. To suggest that all there is to life is the physical is not just denial, but pure foolishness and the practicing Magician knows of this. The most unbelieving skeptic would soon find her opinion changed if she had an out-of-body experience, which I mean in a very literal sense. This practice is also known as *astral projection*.

What is Astral Projection?

Astral projection, also perceived as astral travel, is the act of deliberately leaving your body or moving your consciousness away from the physical onto other realms. This begs the question, what, exactly, is leaving the body? And you might also wonder, where does this thing leave the body for?

You are not your mind, and you are not your body. You are pure consciousness or soul. When you travel the astral plane, what you're doing is turning your consciousness away from the physical plane of existence to the astral one. You may think of your consciousness as your astral body, which takes on the construct of your physical body, or any other form you will find it to take on in the astral plane.

Resist the temptation to think this is all just hogwash. Thanks to the work of scientists and curious minds as Robert Muldoon, there is now more known about the subject of astral travel. It is not mere fiction. It is real, indeed.

Astral projection is an ancient practice, and it cuts across so many cultures. We have the Theosophists of the 19th century to thank for the term "astral projection." This phenomenon often happens with constant meditation and with lucid dreaming. There are those who have managed to achieve astral travel by practicing self-hypnosis or using hallucinogenic substances. There are scientists who classify astral projection as nothing more than pseudoscience, but it is simply their willful ignorance and arrogance that keeps them from exploring a very real, very rich world that exists. Perhaps it troubles them to perceive there are things that cannot be measured using their physical tools.

Why You Should Learn to Astral Project

To properly practice magic, you must be well aware of who you are. This means you must go beyond knowing the physical person that sits right now, reading this book. You must know every aspect of yourself, for only then can you truly be in control of your life. With astral projection, it is easier and easier for you to craft a life in alignment with your True Will.

Astral projection is an excellent tool for encouraging your spiritual growth and the expansion of your awareness or consciousness. It allows you to work on your True Will from a higher plane (or the cause's plane), which affects the physical plane. With astral projection, you will learn the secrets of the universe and the keys to allow you to live an actualized life. It grants you inner vision, peeling back the veil so you can see the worlds beyond this one and gain knowledge that will rapidly advance you in all aspects of life.

While far too many people who think astral projection is a sham, it would be of immense benefit to them to experience it even once. If there's one thing most astral projectors will tell you, it is that they've lost their fear of death. They understand that all that exists is consciousness, so the physical body's death a decay don't mean the conclusion of all life. To look at it logically, if life could "end" or be "taken away," then is it truly *life*? Astral projection allows you to shed all misguided ideas about the human race's fragility and embrace your immortality.

Another argument for making the practice of astral projection a constant in your life is that it is immensely helpful for learning about your past lives, which can give incredible insight into your True Will in your present incarnation. In astral travel, you have access to the Akashic records, which allow you to see the past, the present, and even possible futures as clearly as you see the words on this page.

The Magus knows that astral projection is very important for working on inner planes. This is particularly for serving those in dire need of healing, helping those who are passing on to find peace in the "afterlife," and being a beacon of unity and love for everyone else on higher levels, and so on.

If you hope to reach out to otherworldly beings, be they people who have passed on, angels, spirits, other entities, then you can easily do so through astral travel. You can also visit any spot you want to on Earth and even worlds beyond. You can see friends and even go to places some military won't let you visit... the applications of astral projection are endless.

As you study magic, understand that it is your duty to discover the aspects of you that you haven't yet discovered. You must make conscious that which lies unconscious within you. The summary of the matter is this: To become better than who you are, accept that you are greater than you assume you are. You are beyond physical. You are consciousness. And consciousness is everything, too vast to be contained by a label, a name, or a body.

The Astral Body

You would not be far off to think of the astral body as a vehicle through which you travel around the astral plane. The Magus with clairvoyant sight can perceive it as an aura rich with colors and make of matter of a considerably sharper and finer density than the physical body. The astral body allows desires, emotions, passions, and feelings to be expressed and transmitted between your body and your mind — the latter being of a considerably sharper vehicle than your body.

Everyone has an astral body, but too few people are aware it exists, and fewer still can keep it fully under their control with the fullness of their awareness. You then become the Magus able to keep the astral body in your control, developing it and using it, so you may reap the benefits of the many powers conferred on you.

Everyone projects astrally, whether they remember it or not. The master astral projector has learned to move her astral body at will to wherever she wants it to go. However, others often find themselves in a vague, barely remembered dream because of how primitive and underdeveloped their astral bodies are. They awaken from sleep, clueless about where they have been, what they've done, and who they've met.

When you have developed your astral body through the constant practice of astral travel, while you sleep, you are engaged in meaningful and interesting activities. You do not lose time to slumber because you are still very productive as you move about the astral plane in your astral body. Your days are no longer dull and uninteresting, and your nights are not lost to oblivion. You become the ideal, actualized magician living in a continuous, unbroken cycle of consciousness.

The astral body can travel great distances in just a moment. You could say it moves at the speed of thought. You could be on the other end of the Earth, or the Universe, in a flash.

All emotions and feelings are within your astral body. You must learn to interpret what makes up this body, as this is the key to unlocking your psyche's aspects that have remained hidden from you till this point. There is no better way to understand this aspect of yourself than to practice astral projection and hone your skills so that you're not only able to travel and explore but to remember every experience when you wake up and take up consciousness in the physical realm.

The Qabalah and the Tree of Life

The Tree of Life is a very useful tool that helps to organize a set of mystical concepts.

It is made of 10 spheres, also known as emanations or sephiroth (singular, sephira). These are all connected to one another by 22 paths. Planets are used to symbolize the sephiroth, while the paths are represented by the Hebrew alphabet and divided into the four classical elements, the twelve Zodiac signs, and the seven classical planets. In Western magic, the Tree is used as a filing system, with each path and sephira being assigned an idea, whether that form is a Tarot card, an element, a sign, or a god, among other things.

As for Crowley, it is essential for the magus to understand the Tree of Life. As he writes in Magic Without Tears: *"The Tree of Life has got to be learned by heart; you must know it backward, forwards, sideways, and upside down; it must become the automatic background of all your thinking. You must keep on hanging everything that comes your way upon its proper bough."*

Just like Yoga, the need to learn about the Tree of Life isn't just about magic. It's about being able to know, inside and out, your spiritual blueprint. You can use the Tree to figure out where you want to travel astrally, decide which god you want to invoke, and so on.

Astral Projection Methods

There are several methods for you to will your astral body out and into the astral plane. Some people accomplish this through lucid dreams, where they learn they are dreaming and then project themselves out of their dreams and into the astral plane. Others use drugs to achieve astral projection — though I must warn that you would do well to stay away from this route. It is important for you to be completely in charge of your faculties and not under the influence of substances that can take away from your experience or lead you down undesired paths.

With that said, we'll have a look at the methods you can use to begin astral projection the right way, but first, we'll get into the preparations you need to make to learn astral travel.

Dream Recollection

For you to be a successful astral projector, you need to improve your dream recollection. For most people, when they wake up in the morning, they are quick to forget most details about their dreams, if not all of them. Maybe you can relate to this.

To increase your dream recollection, the first thing you should do is intend to recall your dreams each night when you go to bed. If you often wake up to use the bathroom during the night, you can set this intention to summon your dreams each time. You could either tell yourself mentally or out loud, "I will remember all my dreams tonight," then go to bed knowing you will. Do this night after night, and your memory will improve.

Another thing you absolutely must do is get a journal for your dreams. The very act of writing your dreams down does two essential things: First, it tells your subconscious mind that remembering your dreams is meaningful to you now, and so it should do all it can to help you retain those memories. Next, it helps you see a pattern emerge in your dreams so that the next time you're dreaming, you're more likely to become aware that it's all a dream when "illogical" things happen ... like a man on a cotton candy cloud in the sky saying the temperature is a nice, green unicorn.

Typically, when you dream, nonsensical things like the previous example don't make much of a blip in your mind. In real life you might stop to ask, "What's going on? Why is there a man in the sky? How is he riding a cloud? How come the cloud is cotton candy? What kind of temperature is a 'nice, green unicorn?" In your dream, you wouldn't bother because your critical thinking abilities have gone to sleep on you.

So, as you note your dreams in your journal, you will become aware of the irrationality of it all, and the next time you have something odd happen in a dream, you're more likely to become lucid. The more you become lucid, the more in charge you will be of your mental processes. The more lucid you become, the more you'll be able to remember, and the better your dream recall, the higher your chances of achieving astral travel.

Astral Projection Techniques

Technique #1: Consciousness Transfer. Make sure you're in your quiet space, alone, so no one can bug you. Dress comfortably and make sure the room is at a temperature where you won't feel too warm or too cold. Now, sit or lie in a comfortable position in which you can remain relaxed for an hour. Adjust as needed right away, so you don't make adjustments that jolt you out of your altered state later.

Now, shut your eyes and breathe in deep and slow, allowing all physical tension, negative emotions, thoughts, and intentions to melt away from you with each breath. If this is your first time, you may need about ten or twenty minutes to do a body scan. Start from the top of your head to the soles of your feet, progressively relaxing each body part and imagining a warm, soothing wave of relaxation undoing all tense knots in your body. Do not rush this process.

When you feel well relaxed and at peace, you may now count down from ten to one or chant a mantra for as long as you need until you get into a state of altered consciousness. Don't worry about needing the state to be deep. You'll find over time that *lighter is better.*

Now it is time to build your astral body or your light body. Know the form you want it to assume. You can keep it simple and let it adopt the same form as your physical body. Imagine this body coming together bit by bit, just a few feet away from where your physical body rests.

Next, you must project into this light body your mental energy and energy you draw either from the sky or from the earth. This way, your energy isn't depleted, and you can use the energy abundant in nature to create what you desire. All you must do is mentally connect with the earth or the sky and then see that stream of energy moving from either of those into the light body you're charging. Forget about obstructions like the ceiling or walls or the floor, as those cannot stand in the way of divine energy. If you can't stop being distracted by them, you can create a hole in the ceiling or wall or floor in your mind's eye and see the energy move through it. In time, you will realize this is unnecessary. Do not be shocked to find that the concept of time has lost all meaning. Allow the process to take place with no worries about time.

When your light body has become stable and solid to you, mentally assign its duty to it. You are responsible for this body, and you must dismantle this body when it has achieved its purpose so it doesn't follow you around till it's drained or cause issues for other astral travelers.

Tell the light body what you want it to do. Do not use flowery language. Be as direct and literal as you can be, and back up the words of power with images in your mind for what you expect it to achieve. After doing this, it's time to move your consciousness to the light body. Shift your awareness from your physical body to your light body. Do not do this by literally stepping out of your body; simply imagine that you are looking through your light body's eyes and feeling yourself standing where it stands. Keep your attention there for as long as possible.

Don't try to move from that spot. Simply allow your consciousness to look around the room from that one spot. If you move before you're ready, you will wind up back in the physical and have to begin the process again. Once your consciousness is stable, you can will your light body anywhere. You don't have to walk out a door or move through the ceiling or walls. You can *will* yourself wherever you want to go, and you'll be there.

When you're done exploring, get back to where you made the light body, then allow your consciousness to head back to your physical body, by simply willing it in your mind. Dismantle your light body by imagining it dissipating into nothingness, or you can imagine the light body being reabsorbed into yours so you retain all your energy and have an even better memory of all you did.

Technique #2: Travel by Meditation. Find a quiet place where you will not be disturbed and where you don't have to worry about someone walking in on you. This concern can hamper your ability to relax. Quiet is very important for you to practice, especially as a beginner successfully. Over time you can project regardless of the surrounding noise.

Make sure your body is nice and warm when you astral project. If it's too cold, you cannot remain in your meditative state unless you're an advanced practitioner. Cover up with an afghan or something and wear loose clothing or remain in the nude beneath the covers. You may sit up or lie down. If sitting, keep your spine straight to allow energy flow. If lying down, ensure you're practicing at a time when you will not fall asleep, so you can project. Be able to continue in this position for at least an hour without feeling uncomfortable.

Shut your eyes, take slow, deep breaths, and exhale all tension and stress out of our body. Do a slow body scan and get rid of all pressure by imagining a wave of relaxation undoing those knots. Progressively relax your whole body from head to toes.

Once you are totally relaxed, enter your altered state of consciousness by counting down from ten to one using the visualization technique we covered in an earlier chapter. Go as deep as feels natural to you and do your best to keep your mind from wandering to mundane stuff. If you don't, you'll just fall asleep. You can avoid this by saying a mantra or word repeatedly while imagining an object as simple as a square or triangle or whatever shape you want. This way, your mind has something to focus on.

When your body goes numb, resist the temptation to move or twitch or flex anything. Notice the feeling or urge to do so and then release it. Let your mind drift on to seeking depth: no sight, no sound matters. This is the point where you'll feel a swaying sense on the inside or where you'll see much colored lights on the screen of your inner eyes. Do not attempt to force yourself out of your body. Just let your consciousness separate from your body when it is ready. Your only job is to be as detached from everything as possible, keeping control of the whole experience with a forceless will.

It will soon occur to you that you can see the room around you or that you can see another environment near you. This means you've astral projected. Remain there for a moment and make mental notes of all you can see and hear, so you can check its veracity later. When you move, only to find yourself back in your body, simply will your consciousness back out to the place where it was. Don't try to go to some other place for now. Let it go back to where it knows. You might need a few more sessions to gain the ability to take your astral body wherever else. Just give it time.

Ready to end your projection? Move your consciousness back to your physical body by becoming aware of it. Count forward from one to ten, gradually returning to normal consciousness. Slowly allow yourself to become cognizant of the body, noticing your head, neck, chest, belly, thighs, calves, and feet. Gently flex your feet and hands as you open your eyes, nice and slow. Don't get up too fast. Give yourself time to get used to the physical.

Remember: You must journal your experiences. Notice what worked, what went wrong, and how you can adjust during your next session.

Chapter Six: Building Your Sacred Space

If you truly intend to practice magic, you need to create a sacred space dedicated to your practice. Having this space primes you to move to a state of mind that allows you to express the power within you. You know when you're there that you must clear your mind and allow the divine to come through you.

Your Altar

Think of your altar as your sacred workspace, where you perform your magical rituals. The altar is also where you keep all the tools you need for your magical practice, and all things that represent the purpose or theme of the rituals you conduct. Most religious, magical, and spiritual ceremonies involve the use of altars. Humans have always set up altars for their religious and spiritual ceremonies, across religions and cultures, whether it's a pile of bricks, a table set in the center of the room, or in a corner.

You can choose an altar that is practical and simple, or one that is extravagant and a lovely sight. At the end of the day, your altar, which is a table or a platform, is the place you treat with the utmost honor, devotion, and respect. You allow nothing or anyone to desecrate it. You can place both functional and symbolic items, representative of the deities and spirits you honor. At your altar, you meditate, chant, say your prayers, cast your spells, and do any other rituals you must.

When you keep the altar sacred and pure, you are basically keeping an open door for the energies you work with to come through and concentrate in that area, working with you as you set your intentions, perform your rituals, or celebrate your manifestations.

You will find the altar to be of many benefits to you for expressing gratitude for your blessings, exploring your creative side, seeking guidance, fostering spiritual growth, and going on a deeper and deeper exploration of your true self.

You may wonder if an altar is necessary for your practice. First, you must answer a few questions about magic. Is it something you're genuinely interested in? Do you find that you're usually performing your rituals in a specific room or area? Do you find that your decorations change along with the seasons? If your answer to even one of these questions is yes, then you just might find having an altar will be of immense benefit to you. However, you don't have to have one. In the end, it's your choice. You know within you whether you must have an altar.

Creating Your Altar

You must first decide on the location of the altar. Where do you want it to be? Ideally, it should be a part of your home where you will not be disturbed, whether indoors or outdoors. You must also consider the type of surface you intend to use and where it would be most ideal for you to carry out your magical work in your chosen space.

The location of the altar can also depend on the main intention behind your magical rituals. For instance, if you're working with Aphrodite, the goddess of love, then you might find it best to set up your altar in your bathroom or your bedroom. If you're working with deities or spirits for abundance, then it would make sense to place your altar in the dining room, or in the kitchen, as a symbolic representation of feasting, abundance, warmth, security, and all else tied in with your intentions.

You need not use any super fancy material to serve as the surface. Whether it's a plastic table, a concrete slab, a wooden plank, or whatever, you just want it to be somewhere; it will not be disturbed. Pay special attention when you clean out the space where your alter will be, so you get rid of negative or old, stagnant energy before it's all set up. You may burn sage while chanting a mantra to clear out unwanted energy.

Next, you must think about what goes on your altar. For starters, if it is your desire, you could place an altar cloth over your altar. This clarifies it to your mind and all present energies this space is designated for holy work. You can also take advantage of the magic of color by choosing a color that represents your intention and will supercharge it. If your magical ritual is for love, try a deep red. If it's for abundance, see how green works to supercharge your ritual. If you seek the peace of mind, try a nice calming blue. For increased spiritual growth and insight, seek lavender or purple.

Besides the altar cloth, you will need objects that represent the four elements and/or the four directions. Using lit candles will represent the element of fire, and the south; using a bowl of water will represent the west, and the water element; feathers can represent air and the east, while a bowl of salt (or Earth) will represent the north, and the Earth element. You may choose other objects to signify these things; remember that your practice is personal. Follow your intuition, and you won't be steered wrong.

Another object you will need is a representation of the deity or spirit with which you'll be working. Black candles are used to work with God's energy, while white candles are used to work with Goddess energy. You can also use statues, symbols, pictures, or whatever else you intuitively feel is most representative of the deity.

Use crystals and special stones to supercharge your magic and amplify your intention. Various crystals have various purposes, so pick something that will serve your intention and increase your magical work success. To take things up a notch, consider lighting incense and making use of essential oils. These will help you set the mood for your magical work and will cause you to be more grounded by working with your sense of smell. They also are very effective in cleansing bad energy.

Finally, you'll need your journal, or a grimoire, or a book of shadows. In this book, you'll have records of all your rituals, spells, recipes, lunar events, and notes on your experiences or insights you received during or after performing your ritual. Set your journal on your altar, so it's easy to use, and its intention is very clear for magic only.

If you're working with a deity, or spirit, or god, or the soul of a dearly departed one, then you should have objects representative of them on the altar. Do the proper research so you know the best symbols to use and so your rituals feel very authentic to you.

Care for Your Altar

Each day, you must make sure you work with your altar, or that you work around it at least. Light up the candles. Do you have flowers there? Change them as soon as they die and keep the water fresh. Make sure everything remains in its place. Treat it as you would a live, sacred deity. You often invoke a lot of energy from your altar, so you want to make sure that it's always just right and that you don't ignore it either.

Whenever you invoke a deity, it is in your best interest to do something that shows your gratitude to them. You could present them an offering from nature, or you could bake something that is made with herbs that deity resonates with. If you can't do that, you could sit for a few minutes, simply saying "Thank you" repeatedly, and feeling appreciation for them wash over you.

Cleansing Your Altar's Space

Your altar will give you a form of focus, so you can channel your spiritual intentions as pure as possible. It allows you to do your prayers and affirmations with a sense of clarity and with clean, potent energy. It should be the place you go when you need to recharge, recalibrate, and ground yourself anew. Therefore, it's so important that you consecrate the space you choose and keep it holy.

To cleanse the area, you must first sweep it. Once it's nice and clean, you can then begin the process of smudging. Smudging involves burning an herb with cleansing properties. The most favored of all herbs for cleansing is the sage. In the process of living life each day, energy can gather and stagnate, and this stagnant energy is of no good to you when you're practicing your magical rituals. Smudging is a very ancient ceremony where plants like tobacco, sage, and sweetgrass are burned. This smoke gets rid of all negative ions in the space, and then it allows blessings to flow through the environment so things can become new and dynamic again. Smudging is simply giving your space a reboot and re-energizing. It's a process that even removes any bacteria that might be in the air.

To smudge your sacred space, you'll need sage. This symbolizes the element of earth. When burned, its smoke symbolizes the element of air. You'll also need an abalone shell in which to place the sage or whatever holy plant you're working with, so you can burn it safely. The abalone shell represents the element of water. If you don't have access to a shell, you may simply hold the smudge stick with your fingers.

You've obviously got to have a box of matches or a lighter. This will represent the element of fire. A feather will be needed to represent the air element. When you don't have a feather, you can simply wave your smudge stick about, allowing the smoke to represent the element of air.

It helps to have sacred drums or sacred percussive music, which will represent the heartbeat. If you don't have access to drumming music or drums, you can simply make a clear intention about your heartbeat, and then imagine there is drumming going on. You must trust in magic to create the sounds for you.

What to Do When There's No Room

You may live in a home where there's barely enough room for you to have an altar, or there are too many people in every room, and it just means you will have no privacy. If the former situation is your case, then don't worry about having a dedicated space to perform your magic. This can be to your advantage.

Even if the only space you have to yourself right now is your bed, you can make the process of clearing the energies and setting up all your magical tools a part of your ritual. Think of it as preparing your mind to deal with the mystical, even as you prepare your bed for the same thing. If you're worried about using your bed, especially when using candles, then you can simply clean a good spot on the floor and then set up your tools there.

If you live in a home with just too many people, consider performing your rituals during the night when everyone else has gone to bed. You can also simply find a suitable spot outside for you to set up your altar and begin your magical rituals.

If you have no other options, then remember that magic is magic. It is not limited by the presence or absence of an altar. You can still perform your rituals and do your meditations. If you feel that having an altar will prepare you, then you can imagine that where you are is holy ground, for it truly is. You can also hold on to an object, like a crystal or a stone, and allow that be what you use to center you and ground you so you can work with the energies you require as you do your magic.

Magic that won't work without the presence of all these tools and altars aren't magic to begin with. The purpose these things serve is to help put you in a state of mind where you can easily focus on your intentions. The more you practice — particularly meditation — the more you'll realize that wherever you are in the moment is a sacred space. The divine is not limited by the physical. Remember that.

Chapter Seven: The Tools of the Craft

There are certain devices that, while not necessary, can help the practitioner of magic. When you set up your practice, begin with the devices that have historically proven to be very effective for others who began their magical journey before you. Then adjust as needed, as you find a magical philosophy that matches your personality and lifestyle. Try to remember that there is no such thing as a right or a wrong way of going about your magical practice. Simply go along with what you feel in your soul to be perfect for you.

Be open to experimenting with new tools, yourself, or others who share a love for and understanding of magic.

Magical tools often correspond with the four elements and the four directions.

- **The North/The Earth:** Represented by the Pentacle and Salt. Meaning "To Know."

- **The South/Fire:** Represented by the Blade and the Candle. Meaning "To Dare."

- **The East/Air:** Represented by the Wand and Incense. Meaning, "To Will."

- **The West/Water:** Represented by the Chalice and the Cauldron. Meaning, "To Keep Silent."

Now let's sink our teeth into the tools of the magical trade.

The Altar: We've already covered this. It's where you do most of your magical work. On the altar, there is typically a representation of the four elements and the four directions. You can also find pictures of one's ancestors, representations of spiritual beings in the form of a statue or a painting, a censor used for burning incense, an offering bowl, crystals, stones, amulets, and whatever is important to the Magus.

The Athame: This is a ceremonial blade that customarily has a black handle. This dates to the Middle Age grimoire known as the Key of Solomon. You'll also see mention of fit in the 1950 works of Gerald Gardner. The *athame* is for channeling and directing more powerful energies, which are basically etheric fire. Usually, the blade is left unsharpened and will have some iron to keep all evil entities away during a ritual.

It is connected to the element of fire because of the forge's heat. There are traditions that insist the athame is of the air element. However, it is still a powerful tool you can use to make the spirits or elements do your bidding, as it also connotes an air of threat when you wield it during a ritual.

The Bell: This bell is a great tool for clearing out all negative energy in a space or around an object or a person. It also works to prepare the mind, putting it in the headspace for the magical rituals about to take place. The same can be said of any musical instrument used during a ritual. When the bell rings, it grabs the attention of helpful divine entities to fortify your intention and help you see it through.

The Besom: This is a broom, historically known as the witch's broom. This can be a source of inspiration or terror. The old Witches would concoct flying potions using the most dangerous of hallucinatory ingredients, and they would take flight under the influence of their magical potions on their brooms. The broom is a tool and a symbol for cleansing, physically and magically, and is used to purify the sacred space for your ritual. If you put it above your new home's door, it will keep out all negative entities and all bad luck. However, as you move to a different home, you must have a fresh broom. Do not carry the old one with you.

The Book of Shadows: This is a book that has been made by hand, and is filled with every recipe, spell, ritual, and mystical knowledge from a coven of witches or from a solo practitioner of magic.

The Boline: This tool has a white handle, and it's a favorite of witches and gardeners as well. It has serrations on the inner blade that are very helpful for making wands. The sharp exterior edge does a great job of cutting plants and dicing them into bits.

The Chalice: This vessel contains spiritual energy and usually holds wine within it. When the practitioner offers a guest to drink of this wine, it is a symbolic invitation to partake in the blessings that accrue from the ritual. In Wicca, the male athame is inserted into the female chalice to symbolize sexual intercourse, or the "Great Rite." This is balancing the masculine and the feminine and the energy of procreation and regeneration.

The Candles: These are perfect for giving your magical work a good charge. Historically, the flame is regarded as a spark of life force or source energy. It symbolizes the divinity of communication, and it is the fire element itself, which brings about spiritual and physical change. The candle is your life energy and mental power extended, allowing you to project your will into the universe and to your spirit guides for it to be manifested.

The Cauldron: Historically, the cauldron was a cast-iron pot that our ancestors used for cooking. In some parts of the world, the cauldron is still used for cooking. This is a very vital magical tool. When performing scrying rituals burning rituals that lead to transformation, and when directing our will toward specific intentions, the cauldron represents all the elements. Its round shape is a representation of the earth or mother nature. Its three legs represent water, as the maiden, or the mother crone, or the phases of the moon. The fire beneath it is revered for its transformational power, and the smoke or steam that rises off the cauldron represents the air element.

The Censer: This is where incense is burned. There are people who use a thurible instead. The smoke you see from the burning incense will take your spiritual messages and intentions to the divine beings you have chosen to work with. Many kinds of incense have specific ingredients that help with certain rituals, so you will need to do your homework to discover which kind you should work with at any point in time. A censer is basically a safe place for you to burn your chosen incense. The thurible is a kind of censer that hangs from a chain you can carry around or that lets you swing the incense back and forth as you cleanse your space.

The Clothing: Not just any clothing. This is the ritual attire, which is very vital for a lot of magic practitioners. Historically, witches would put on dark, black cloaks at night so the public eye would not fall upon them and so they would not be persecuted for practicing their magic.

You will need to have an article of clothing - be it a shirt, a tunic, skirt, hat, or a special pair of gloves or pants - which you only ever use during the performance of rituals. In time, you will find that wearing this item will put you in a magical frame of mind as soon as you've got it on, so you don't have to spend time meditating or breathing, trying to find the perfect frame of mind to begin your great work.

The Crystals: There are all sorts of crystals, but each is powerful for bringing about the change you seek in your life. Crystals remind the magician when she wears or carries them around of her intention and what she intends to see come to pass in her life. The subtle energies that emanate from the crystals merge with your energy and will assist you with anything you're doing in life. They will often have the property of the elements of life. For instance, agate portrays the earth, aquamarine represents water, citrine suggests fire, and lepidolite means air.

The Divinatory Items: These items allow you to gain rare insight into whatever burning questions or matters you have on your mind from a supernatural standpoint. There are tools to divine the answers. These include runes, oracle cards, animal omens, alomancy (also called "spilled salt"), aeromancy (using the weather), ogham, melted wax, dowsing, tarot, spirit boards, ashes, crystals, I Ching, numerology, pyromania, astrology, bibliomancy (books) and so much more.

The Grimoire: This is a record of all things magical, including your experiments, your thoughts, and the clear guidance you have received on how to carry out your rituals. Whether yours or another's, the grimoire will often have precise instructions that show you how to invoke an angel or a demon, how to gain and develop your spiritual powers, and how to perform divination properly. Grimoires have been in circulation throughout Europe ever since the Middle Ages, despite the Church's desperate undertaking to burn all things it considered occult.

Back in those times, it was vital for the practitioner of magic to keep their grimoires well-hidden to avoid being persecuted by the Christian church or burned at the stake. We've come a long way since then, and you can now safely have your grimoire wherever is most convenient for you — preferably right on your altar so that you can easily refer to it during your rituals as needed.

The Offering: You'll need an offering bowl. It doesn't matter what material it is made of. The whole point behind this is to put in offerings that are symbolic and will be appreciated by the deity you're working with.

The Oils: Magical oils make your rituals more potent than ever and will help you remember your goals as you perform your magical exercises. You can use these oils for candle magic, meditation, charge your amulets and other tools, spiritual cleansing, making potions, anointing or healing another, and more. You want to ensure you only use the natural oils and stay away from the chemical ones in every corner of the market these days. You want to make sure your magical oils are natural, essential oils.

The Pentacle, or the Pentagram: Across every ancient culture, from Greece to Egypt, the Latin America Mayans to India, and even China, the five-pointed star or the pentagram has always been viewed as a powerful, potent, and ever-present symbol in the history of humanity. You'll discover it etched on caves from the Neolithic era. You'll notice it in drawings from ancient Babylon, showing Venus on its astrological journey. You'll find pentagrams in Hebrew scripture as well.

Whether you call it the pentacle or the pentagram, they mean the same thing. It is a talisman that every magic practitioner would do well to own if they can. If you wear a pentacle, it protects you from bad luck and negative experiences. It will chase away all evil entities and bring the good ones close to you so that they're willing to aid you in all your endeavors. The pentacle also represents all five of the classical elements: Earth, Water, Fire, Air, and Ether (or spirit). Usually, the one solitary point on the pentacle is placed upwards, representing the human form, and the entire star is usually within a circle, which represents protection and a mastery of all four elements by the spirit of the wearer.

The Scrying Bowls: These scrying bowls give you with spiritual insight and allow you to see visions. You can use them with water, fire, smoke, or any other substance on hand.

The Staff: Where it's not legal for you to use blades, you can use a staff instead. With the staff, you show you are connected to the earth. The staff has been used for the centuries by Shamans, who are very connected themselves. In certain spring ceremonies, it is also used to wake the Earth, the Great Mother, from the slumber of winter, by gently beating it on the ground. You may decorate your staff and charge it with magical symbols, runes, crystals, amulets, oils, and herbs. It can also be manipulated in place of a wand.

The Wand: This is a thin rod you hold in your hand, generally made of wood, crystal, ivory, stone, or precious metals like silver and gold. The magus uses the wand to channel energy as needed. The athame is often used to issue commands, the wand is used in a much gentler manner to encourage all entities and energies to grant your intentions peacefully. Wiccans see the wand as a representation of the air element. Other traditions see it as a symbol of fire instead.

The wand is used to point your attention towards whatever you want to will into the world. It communicates clearly what your Will in any situation. Use it to channel healing energy to others or to yourself. You can manipulate the wand to implant a set purpose into a talisman, crystal, candle, amulet, or any other magical object you're working with. With it, you can softly encourage spiritual energies you desire to come to your aid. You can use your wand for fishing out any energy blockage in a place or in the body and remove them. Or you can use it to open your chakras, or those of another; create portals which will connect you to otherworldly realms, and even pass along your will to your helpful spiritual guides.

The Most Powerful Tool of All

One tool determines the effectiveness of all other tools. You can't find it in a shop, nor can you buy it, I'm afraid. This tool isn't even it. Well , , , what is "it?"

In a word: You!

While every magical tool has its importance and possesses its very own vibration, which continues to grow stronger and stronger with prolonged use, your spirit is most vital in your rituals. These tools are lifeless in and of themselves. What powers them is simply your Will and intention, your constant use of and practice with them.

It is always important that, you perform your rituals from a place of pure love and true compassion for everyone else, with the intent that no harm comes to you or anyone involved directly or indirectly.

Create techniques that work well for you, though they might differ from what others are engaged in. Remember that you have your own special path, your own True Will. When things do not turn out as you'd like, or your intention doesn't come to pass in the ways you'd prefer, or as at the time you'd have preferred, what you've got to do is keep adjusting as your intuition leads you to, until you become better. Continue practicing until your practice becomes a habit you engage in on autopilot, wherever you are, no matter the circumstances. Again, magic is not dependent on objects or environments. True magic lies within you.

I leave you with this final, very important note before we move on to the next chapter: Do not fall into the trap of ascribing power to the items outside of you. They are tools and nothing more. The hand has the authority, not the hammer in hand. It will only do as the hand directs it. If the hand does nothing with the hammer, then the hammer is just another useless thing. Do not give away your power to that which is lifeless. Take responsibility for your life and your manifestations.

Chapter Eight: Preparing for Ritual

Practicing magic effectively means that the magician must participate in some form of ritual to give his intentions clear direction and have a distinct focus on what energy to draw and where to direct it.

What's A Ritual?

It is basically a process or a whole sequence of various activities, which include actions, words, gestures, and objects. These exercises are carried out in a sacred, consecrated space and will always follow a specific order.

They are more common than you think. Even singing the national anthem before a football match is a ritual on its own. Typically, it will have formality to it, and it's often rooted in ancient traditions. No one strays from the set sequence, as there are rules that must be followed to the letter. You'll also find that most of them involve a lot of symbolism and performance as well.

There are all sorts of rituals, from religious sacraments to worship rites, purification rites to rites of passage, atonement rites, coronations, dedications, marriages, presidential inaugurations, funerals, and more.

Elements and Components of Rituals

Formalism: They are often set according to strict codes that give no room for improvisation or deviation. The element of formalism shows up in the way the magician and other participants speak during the sacred event. There's a certain intonation, series of words, volume, and order, inducing a mood of magic and acceptance in all who partake.

Traditionalism: They are often based on ancient, age-old traditions. It is important to remain true to the original form of the ritual as much as possible for it to have meaning and to achieve the desired aftermath.

Consider the well-known Thanksgiving dinner, a good old-fashioned American ritual, with its origins from America's Puritanical settlement.

Invariance: All rituals leave no room for alteration. There is a deliberately orchestrated series of movements or choreography. It will compel you to discipline your body to mold your mind into a condition suitable for magic.

Rule Governance: They have rules by which they are governed. Like the element of formalism, rules instill certain norms and checks to make sure that all behavior conforms to the mood of the group. The guidelines clarify it what is acceptable or not.

Sacrifice: Magic, by its very definition, has rituals that are supernatural in nature. When working with particular deities, angels, demons, or other entities, there will usually be a need for sacrifice. This does not necessarily mean that one needs to make blood sacrifices or anything of the sort; it can simply be enough that you make sure there are symbols that represent you choosing to give – or "sacrifice" – and you're mindfully allowing the forces that need to work on your behalf the freedom to do so.

Performance: They are often like an actual stage performance. It has a spirit of theater, and rightly so, considering that every element and object used during one is symbolic, representing something else. They all have meaning, which must be enacted by the magician.

The Importance of Rituals

Whether it's your secular life or your sacred life, they matter. Even the way you begin your day, the way you get to work, and the way you handle holidays or resumption of your duties are rituals. They connect the past to the present and the present to the future. They perceive continuity and bring about order to our lives.

Magical rituals take you away from the secular and mundane to the magical space. All the sequences involved in one work hand in hand to generate the energy you need and then release that same energy with laser-like precision to help you achieve your goal.

The human is a creature of habit, so not surprisingly, we find a lot of safety and comfort in our rituals. We have a sense of dependability and can trust that things will work out a certain way, regardless of the apparent chaos in the outside world. They let you know where you belong in all the seemingly randomness of life.

Embedded in them are a lot of history and cultures, all of it reflecting the beliefs of magicians from the past till now. Think of it as a spiritual manual which has the blueprint of the magical life. As a magic practitioner, you have a goal or a wish you want to be reflected in you by the universe. All the elements, and the words, choreography, environment, and objects used, have the singular purpose of raising your energy and channeling it towards the thing you desire, making you become part and parcel of the present magic.

For the Magus, they are all about fulfilling her True Will. As she conducts her ritual, she marries the fleeting and the lasting together in the here and now. She melds into the divine and brings the timeless and unseen by the masses right before her very eyes.

They allow you the space you need to channel even more energy than you could through any other means and then actively send that energy out to fulfill your bidding.

Preparing for Your Ritual

As a magician, one of the first things you must do is to take care of your immediate surroundings. If you don't have that much sorted out, how do you plan on directing the energies and forces of nature? You must make sure that your space, as it is, is suitable for magical work.

Wherever you choose to have it will affect the results you get. So, it's best to make use of spaces that allow for energy flow. Consider doing yours outside, or imagine that the energy of nature flows unimpeded to the space you're using indoors. Ideally, performing them in nature is a good way to go, as it allows you and other participants to recognize that we're all woven into the same tapestry.

You may find that you're a bit limited in your choice of location. Do not let that affect you. Simply work with what you've got. You want to make sure that the space you choose can hold you and anyone else who's participating in it.

You want to perform yours in a space you have saged and consecrated for the purpose. You don't want interruptions, distractions, or anything that could take away from the quality and the focus required. You will also want to make sure there are no cell phones or tablets nearby. To set the mood, you can use aromatics, trinkets, and things of that nature.

All seasonal rituals will usually have symbols and decorations that represent that particular season. For instance, an Ostara ritual would benefit from fresh blossoms. You want to choose good music, appropriate incense, and the objects that match the theme of yours. These will play a huge part in affecting your perception, putting you in a magical frame of mind.

As for personal preparations, you must be in the right frame of mind. The same goes for everyone else who joins in. The reason is that everyone's thoughts and emotions will combine, and this energy will feed the group. Everyone must set aside all unimportant and mundane problems and concerns so everybody has the same focus and intention.

Ritual baths before the ceremony are helpful, as they can help cleanse any lingering, old, undesired energy and keep that from tainting your intention. You'll want to add salt to your bathwater – as salt symbolizes purification. You could also add natural, essential oils. If you can, bathe in the ocean, or a lake or stream. Otherwise, don't sweat it. Just take a bath where you can before yours begins.

If you're performing one with others, you'll want to be in a circle. This represents that each person present is responsible for the events that take place, and everyone is equally relevant. All participants must be very clear in their understanding about the reason you've all gathered and should be ready, willing, and able to give of their energy, physically and psychically, so the purpose of it will be fulfilled. If anyone cannot keep their energy positive and clear, then it would be in the interest of all for them to leave. The last thing you need is a weak link who will derail it.

Finally, all ritual objects and tools must be cleansed beforehand. Energetically charge each object so it performs its designated task. Gather every tool you need, and only then should you cast a circle.

The Progression of the Ritual

Every ritual has a progression, with each step being exactly where it is in the sequence of events for a very good reason. Think of them as well-structured plays. You don't want to mess with the orders of the scenes; otherwise, all meaning will be lost.

They all have their very specific beginnings, which will involve creating the sacred environment in which remaining events will occur. The start of your ritual will dictate how the rest of it will go. It takes every participant to the mental space they need to be, transporting them to the point between the physical and the spiritual, where all is one. It unites everyone in spirit and mind so they can focus on the intention for which all have gathered with one collective heart.

At the start of it, you can have all participants breathe together at the same pace while linking their hands and calling on all deities and angels that need to be present. If you're a magician practicing solo, you will need a moment to pray or meditate and invoke the circle.

Once you've arrived at the point of harmony, what happens next will depend on the goal. You might weave spells, sing, drum, or dance. You could sit in meditation, or visualize, engage in divinations, or even enact a symbolic event. Whatever you do choose should match with your intention.

Remember that the more you involve the senses, the more you will raise the energy needed to make yours a success. This means burning incense, incorporating music, and things of that nature. You will notice that as the energy rises, the drumming or chanting might become faster and louder. This is a good thing.

The end of it is just as important as the beginning. It helps to have a solid finish, one that will direct all magicians' attention back to the regular, mundane things of life. If it doesn't have a proper ending, it will be like a bad cliffhanger in a TV show. The participants will have a sense of incompleteness, and the intention of it may remain unfulfilled.

You must have an end to your ritual, which includes acknowledging your desire has been accomplished and releasing all spirits and deities summoned to assist you with it. Also, all participants must ground themselves. When done, deconstruct your circle, say a prayer of thanks, or end with a chant. Each participant must accept the knowledge it is complete and that the intention is sent forth and shall not return unfulfilled.

Chapter Nine: Performing Purification

Staying clean and pure is very vital for every magical act. This is why there are purification rites.

Purification

Purification is the process of setting yourself free and clear of all that is unclean, especially before you do anything magical or work with deities and spirits. You must make sure that you are clean, in mind, and in the body.

Purification doesn't just apply to you; it applies to the objects you use during a ritual and the space you're conducting it in. Historically, the phrase "cleanliness is next to godliness" has been used to explain that being pure is something you do not skimp on during your magical practice.

A lot of rituals insisted on cleanliness, even long before the germ theory was discussed. Eastern religions have always valued purity, both physical and mental. To be impure during a ritual was always a taboo. An added benefit of purification practices is that everyone knows they're not at risk of contracting something from the other person.

Impurities range from trash, bodily fluids, and waste to immoral behavior within the context of your magical beliefs.

Purification is almost the same thing as banishing, except it's a lot more rigorous, in that you must prepare not just your temple but yourself to carry out your rituals. According to Crowley, magicians of old often went through very arduous purification methods, fasting, abstaining from sex, going on very special diets, making sure the body remained clean and tidy, and doing a series of very complex prayers.

Don't worry about partaking in all of this, though, because Crowley also says that there's no longer any need for all of that to purify yourself. You can simply set an intention, will yourself to be pure, and that's the end of the matter. This is how you can keep your mind and body pure from all things that would interfere with your spiritual practice. Crowley writes in Magic, Book IV:

The point is to seize every occasion of bringing every available force to bear upon the objective of the assault. It does not matter what the force is (by any standard of judgment) so long as it plays its proper part in securing the success of the general-purpose [...] We must constantly examine ourselves and assure ourselves that every action is really subservient to the One Purpose.

For Crowley, it was enough to participate in symbolically relevant rituals like bathing and robing. Taking a bath is a symbol that shows you have removed everything that is not supportive of your one intention. Putting on your robe also shows that you're donning all that is good and supportive of your intention.

Banishing

Banishing is a ritual that removes all spiritual influences that should not be in the ritual space, from spirits to negative, stagnant energies. A lot of banishing rituals exist, but you can keep it as simple as needed.

Before you cast a circle — which means to draw a magical circle around you and your participants that will channel your energies better and keep you protected — you want to perform this to sanctify the magical area. Banishing is literally casting all unwanted entities and energies away from your space. You'll want to do your banishing as regularly as possible so that your altar and magical work area remain free and clear of negativity and impurity, so you can practice your magic and spells.

Crowley suggests that you do a general banishing and keep it short. Of course, other ceremonies are more elaborate, requiring you to banish everything negative, according to its name. Crowley says you should do your banishing ritual at least once a day, as a true Thelemite.

Staying Clean

You cannot afford to be an unkempt, untidy, and dirty person as a magician in the spirit of cleanliness and purity. You must learn to take care of your things and yourself to the best of your abilities.

All outfits used for magical purposes must be kept clean. You, yourself, must make sure that you're physically clean before you put on these clothes or begin your rituals. Bathe in salt water. Wash your magical apparel in salt water. Cleanse all your crystals, amulets, wands, and other objects using salt water, and with the intention that only positive, helpful energies are imbued in them all.

If it seems to you like overkill, think about how important it is to you that every ritual you do, every intention you put forth, not be a total waste of your time at best, or attract the wrong results and the wrong entities at worst.

Crowley's Lesser Banishing Ritual of the Pentagram

The Lesser Banishing Ritual of the Pentagram, also known as LBRP for short, is a magical ritual used by the Golden Dawn order and is now very popular in modern-day occultism. It is often considered a nonnegotiable starter of all magical work, and so important that as a member of the order of the Golden Dawn, you are taught this first (other than other initiation rituals) before you can join the Inner Order.

The Lesser Banishing Ritual of the Pentagram is incredibly dynamic. It requires gestures, calling out particular power words, visualization, evocation, prayer, and the clearing and preparation of a magical work area to allow you to perform more magic or simply do your meditations.

The point of this ritual is to banish any, and all impure forms, any entities about chaos, and all that doesn't perfectly represent the five classical elements of magic. You will need to use your wand to trace pentacles in the air and then draw on the power of divine entities' names. You'll also need to invoke all spiritual forces in charge of all the elements to keep guard over the circle and keep it fortified.

The Lesser Banishing Ritual of the Pentagram and the Qabalistic Cross have certain basic parts that are credited to Eliphas Levi, a French occultist. The origin of the text was a Jewish prayer traditionally said before going to bed. Of course, this is noted by Rabbi Samson Raphael Hirsch in his book, The Hirsch Siddur (1969). This is how it goes:

In the Name of God, the God of Yisrael: may Michael be at my right hand, Gabriel at my left, Uriel before me, Raphael behind me, and above my head, the presence of God.

Preparing for the Lesser Banishing Ritual of the Pentagram

Certain orders say there is certain magical equipment that will be used to perform the LBRP. However, according to the Hermetic Order of the Golden Dawn, there is no need for any equipment. For clarity, the Hermetic Order of the Golden Dawn (Ordo Hermeticus Aurorae Aureae) is a secret society firmly devoted to studying and practicing all things occult, paranormal, and metaphysical, founder by William Wynn Westcott, William Robert Woodman, and Samuel Liddell Mathers, all Freemasons.

That said, here's an approach you might want to consider when you want to carry out the lesser banishing ritual of the pentagram yourself:

- Setting up an altar in the middle of your space where all the instruments that represent the four elements will be placed.

- Putting on a ceremonial robe, like a tau robe, or any other garment you only use during rituals and is only worn by the magician, you.

- Having a ritual sword, or a dagger (the athame will do here) or a wand, if you prefer. You will use these to make gestures of the various points on the Qabalistic cross, and you'll also need it to draw the pentacles and the circle that connects all points.

The Process

According to the Golden Dawn order, the *Lesser Banishing Ritual of the Pentagram* has three parts which must proceed in the following order:

>1. **The Qabalistic Cross**: This can be repeated when you're done with the LBRP. The whole point of this is to create an astral cross using the magus's body. Each point on the cross will match the Sephiroth of the Tree of Life. (The Sephiroth, which are emanations, are the 10 attributes in the Qabalah through which the Infinite shows itself and continues to create all realms, both physical and metaphysical.)

>2. **The Formulation of the Pentacles/Pentagrams**: You will draw a banishing earth pentacle for the purpose of the Banishing Ritual, or you will invoke a pentacle when doing an Invoking Ritual by drawing the pentacle in the air at the four cardinal points, and calling out the name of God that matches each point: YHVH for the East, ADNI for the South, AHIH for the West, and AGLA for the North. In this portion of the ritual, you either banish or invoke all four elements of Air, Fire, Water, and Earth in that order. Finally, you will connect all four of those pentagrams in a circle, which you draw in the air.

>3. **The Invocation of Deities or Archangels**: At this point, you will call upon the Archangels in the right order: Raphael, Gabriel, Michael, and Auriel (or Uriel), asking for their presence while you see them in your mind's eye at each of the cardinal points.

If you so desire, and the Judeo-Christian names are not your cup of tea, then you may replace names of the archangels, God, and the Qabalistic Cross with your own substitutes. For instance, rather than use the Tree of Life, you may turn to the Chakra system of the East instead. Rather than use the names of God, you may chant your mantras instead. All Thelemic magicians will usually call upon the name Aiwass, from the heart, as they carry out the Qabalistic cross. This shows their continued commitment to the intelligent Liber AL vel Legis, or The Book of the Law, which is the main sacred text of the Law of Thelema. The thing to remember is that magic is personal. Remember: Do What Thou Wilt. Find what resonates with you and use that method.

Chapter Ten: Three Methods of Invocation

Invocation involves calling up a deity or divine being or identifying with it. According to Crowley, two things are critical if you're going to have a successful invocation. First, he says, "inflame thyself in praying," and then he says, "invoke often." As you do your prayers, chants, dance, or singing, or whatever you do to invoke the spirits, you raise your vibration to match theirs, making it even more likely that the invocation will succeed. It's not enough to simply chant or pray; what Crowley means by inflaming yourself with praying is to allow it to set you ablaze. Feel the passion burn in your heart and soul. Feel the fire of the divine spark rise within you as you pray, and you will invoke the deity you need to work with.

Next, he says, "often invoke" because, as with all things, practice makes perfect. The more you invoke, the better you will become at entering the right state of mind for the invocation to occur. Each new session will happen easier and faster than the last because you come into your own as you master the process.

It is Crowley's belief there is no other invocation that is more important even than other magical acts, than invoking your very own secret self, or your Holy Guardian Angel if you prefer. When you have invoked your secret self, it becomes that much easier for you to figure out what your True Will is. Here is Crowley's description of the invocation experience in Magic (Book 4, chapter 15):

> *"The mind must be exalted until it loses consciousness of self. The Magician must be carried forward blindly by a force which, though in him and of him, is by no means that which he in his normal state of consciousness calls 'I.' Just as the poet, the lover, the artist, is carried out of himself in a creative frenzy, so must it be for the Magician."*

Invocation essentially involves calling up the qualities of an entity into you. Mostly, invocation rituals are devotional. You must surrender yourself in worship to the deity so the deity can move and live through you and bless you.

Crowley's Three Methods of Invocation

In the book, Magic (Book 4), Crowley talks about the three major invocation classes. He does state that, in essence, all three of these classes or methods are one and the same. However, each method involves the magician identifying herself with the Deity being invoked.

Method #1: Devotion. Here, the magician will attain alignment with the identity of God through loving surrender. The magical will give up all things irrelevant to a life filled with devotion to this deity and will suppress all illusionary aspects of themselves.

Method #2: Calling Forth. The Magician will be aligned in identity with the deity by giving dedicated attention to the desired aspect of himself that he seeks to invoke.

Method #3: Drama. The Magician's identity aligns with the deity's by way of sympathy. It's not easy for the regular Joe or Jane to just abandon themselves completely as an actor would abandon their real selves for the character they play in a movie, but when the magician is able to do this, they will find this method to be the best and the most effective of all three.

Assumption of Godforms

The assumption of godforms is yet another technique that the magician can use to invoke their god or deity. You have only to use all your imagination to assume that you are a representation of the god you want to identify with. See yourself as the sum total of the idea represented by that god.

A great way to achieve this god identification is to arrange your posture so it is characteristic of the god or spirit you wish to invoke and imagine that the body of this god is melding with yours, enveloping yours, so you become the living embodiment of the god. As you do this, you can chant or "vibrate" the name of that god. Wear it upon you. Let the essence of this god permeate you, mind, body, and soul. Behold, you are god.

Be Prepared

I shouldn't have to mention how important it is for you to be prepared before you attempt to invoke any spirit or deity. You must make sure that you are pure in heart, and your ritual space is ready. The last thing you need is to invoke a mischievous spirit or being instead of the spirit you want to work with.

You must be prepared in mind. All things that are not relevant to the invocation must become unimportant to you. Let it all go completely and focus on the goal you must achieve at the moment.

Do your best to make sure that you are of pure vibration. This will mean smudging the area you intend to do your invocation in. You could also chant as you smudge to raise your vibration and put you in a receptive state of mind for the invocation.

Finally, think about what you want to accomplish as you carry out your invocation ritual. Why are summoning this deity? What would you like to accomplish by allowing this deity's qualities to become your qualities as well? Keep that front and center in your mind, with the complete faith and expectation you will succeed, no matter what it is. Begin with a mood of appreciation, knowing, and trusting that your intentions are already fulfilled. This positive, expectant mindset will make certain you get the results you want, and you are not disappointed or steered off course.

Chapter Eleven: The Art of Divination

Divination Defined

Among the many abilities and talents of the adept is the art of divination. The whole point behind it is to get information that would prove useful to you as a magician in your Great Work, where you finally can transcend yourself.

Outside of what goes on between your ears, there are various kinds of intelligence you can connect with to receive the most amazing and accurate insight and information, using symbology. Divination is all about getting that insight from the realm of infinite intelligence.

Divination vs. Fortune Telling

It is not the same thing as fortune-telling. When you meet a fortune teller, they try to predict what will happen to you in the future. This is different in that it's more about learning about the true nature of a situation or a person. It helps you gain insight into people, things, places, and events, and with this information, you can make better choices for yourself.

There is no lack of methods across cultures and traditions all over the world. In the West, occultists commonly turn to astrology, which involves figuring out the influence of the planets on us. Tarot is a 78-card system, with each card possessing its unique meaning. They also use bibliomancy, picking up a book like the Bible, the Bhagavad-Gita, I Ching, or Liber Legis, and opening it to read random spots, and geomancy, which involves randomly marking the earth or a piece of paper so it creates a combo of 16 patterns.

Divination: Subjective and Personal

You cannot consider it to be a perfect science. Crowley himself states in chapter 18 of Magic (Book 4), "In estimating the ultimate value of a divinatory judgment, one must allow for more than the numerous sources of error inherent in the process itself. The judgment can do no more than the facts presented to it warrant. It is naturally impossible in most cases to make sure that some important factor has not been omitted [...] One must not assume that the oracle is omniscient."

In other words, it comes down to how you interpret a symbol. If working with dreams as a divination process, a fire might symbolize a danger to one magus, but to another, it could mean regeneration or a new beginning. The subjective nature of it remains constant, no matter the medium used, whether it's the Tarot, or Runes, or Scrying.

Practical Divination Exercises

Divination by Scrying

Scrying is also known as oculomancy, crystal gazing, or hydromancy. It is a very old practice of revelation. If you've ever seen a movie scene where a gypsy was looking into a crystal ball, scrying is exactly what she was depicting — except real scrying is not about attempting to see the future. No one can see the future. You can only speculate about it based on the information you currently have.

The origin of the word "scrying" is the Old English descry, which meant "to reveal" or "to make out dimly." Scrying is the process of revealing what is hidden with our inner sight or second sight. This site represents our ability to perceive that which we rarely pick up on using just our five senses.

The first mention of scrying was in the 10th century, in the Shahnameh, Ancient Persian writing. When Christianity became a thing, it outlawed all scrying as "devilish." This is funny because, across all cultures, there has always been some form of this art, from the Egyptians who used oil to gain insight to the Native Americans who used smoke to show them mysteries.

With scrying, you can connect with your unconscious mind and with realms beyond the physical. You can get a handle on who you are and why you are. If you are yet seeking your True Will, then scrying will be of immense benefit to you, helping you pinpoint our desires and aspirations.

How to Scry

    1. Find a quiet place where you can work with no interruptions. Set things up to help you relax so you can easily enter a trance. If it helps to have a dim room, then shut the blinds. If it helps to have light, throw open the shades. You'll want to enter a meditative state before you begin.

    2. Know your intention. This way, you're more than likely to get the answers you want to have. Set your intention firmly in your mind.

    3. Stare into your chosen medium, whether fire, a crystal ball, a mirror, or water. Your trance state may deepen. This is fine. After some time, you will begin to see images. Shadows, shapes, and silhouettes will form. You may see vague images, or you may see vivid flashes. As you see these things, important dates, locations, and times may come to your mind

that relates to your intention. Don't force yourself to see what isn't there. Just let it happen.

4. When you're done, write down everything you saw, and write down the details of how your session went.

It's okay if, at first, you're afraid of what you might see. To deal with this fear, ground yourself so you feel connected to the physical by allowing the energy from the ground to flow up through your feet and the rest of your body, anchoring you. Gently let yourself know just because you see things doesn't mean you've gone mental. Chant the name of a deity who makes you feel safe.

Divination by Dowsing Pendulum

The pendulum shouldn't be overlooked, as it is a powerful way to find the truth about things. It is not only powerful, but it's also easy to create your own at home, with some thread and a key with an eye for you to pass the thread through.

A dowsing pendulum is usually a crystal or a rock you hang on the end of a chain or a string. It gives insight on all levels, whether it's on a spiritual matter, or you must find something that's been buried beneath the floors. It works by connecting you with the Akashic records, which are full of answers to all of life's pressing issues. When you ask a question, your unconscious mind will respond by affecting your fingers nerve endings, and this makes it swing in answer, so your body tells you what you know on the inside.

How to Use the Pendulum

1. Select the right pendulum. Sure, you can make one out of a key and string, but if you need something to help you get into the magical frame of mind, then you should put more thought into what should serve as a proper pendulum. What material do you want it to be made of? To use a crystal, what kind? Think about the power crystal you resonate with the most. You may go to a magic store, hold on to each one available, and see what calls to you the most.

2. Cleanse your pendulum. You want it to be clear of all energy that is stagnant or residual in it. You can cleanse it in salt water, or bury it in the earth for a day, or use a smudge stick. When you intuitively sense it is cleansed, you can then work with it.

3. Develop a relationship with your pendulum. This is a straightforward thing to do, but it will take some time and a lot of commitment, like an actual relationship. You want to learn the language of your pendulum, and you want it to learn the language of your unconscious mind. To make this happen, you must ask it questions. First, breathe deeply so you can be centered and grounded. Next, request support and guidance by praying to your deity, your higher self, or chanting. Ask that you receive the most objective answers and the clearest ones. Finally, ask it a few questions so you can figure out what it means by "yes," "no," and "maybe."

It might say yes by swinging back and forth, not by swinging side to side, or by swinging around clockwise or counterclockwise. To understand what each direction means, you could say it, "Show me yes," then wait to see. Then tell it, "Show me no," and let it show you. Then ask, "Show me maybe," and watch. Then thank it.

Another approach is to ask questions with objective answers, like, "Am I a man or a woman?" or "Is the sky army green or blue?" or "Am I a parent or not?" Then pay attention to the swinging you get with each question. Make sure always to do this exercise or the previous one because it can change the way it says yes, no, or maybe.

4. Question your pendulum once it's ready for use. Make sure you're comfy in your seat. Make sure your arm is stable and supported at the elbow. Hold it nice and loose between your index finger and thumb. Keep just enough grip to keep it from slipping from your grasp. Suggest the question you want

an answer to. You can ask it anything... as long as it's within reason. You could discover whether you should go to an event, see what you feel about something, or decide on a career change. It can help you with everyday problems, relationships, money issues, and spiritual concerns.

Please be wise about how you use your pendulum. Attempt no divination when your mind feels unbalanced or when you're feeling terrible emotionally or physically, as you will get wrong answers. Make sure you're in the right headspace by asking it if it's a good time to proceed.

It should not replace your doctor. If you need health care, please seek a professional. Only practice with it on yourself, not someone else, unless they have given you permission to work with them or on their behalf.

Begin your sessions with an open mind. Get rid of all your biases. If you have a mind that is focused on a subject, this will obviously affect your process.

Know there's only so much it can do for you. You could try it with scrying, runes, or tarot. You can supplement with scrying to check that the information you get from it is true.

Do not be overly reliant on it. It may be great for divination, but the last thing you want to do is make every decision in life-based on which way the pendulum swings. Be careful not to turn it into a crutch. In magic, it is important to be responsible for all your actions and choices and be conscious of your decision-making. Don't ruin your life or someone else's simply because "my pendulum said it was okay." Don't try to pass on your responsibilities to it. Remember, it's a tool. You have the ultimate power, and you alone should take responsibility or blame for your actions as a true Thelemite.

Before each session you should begin by asking:

- Can I ask this question? As in, am I ready for the answer?

- May I ask this question? As in, am I permitted to? This is useful when dowsing or performing divination for someone else. Also, just because they insist you should ask doesn't mean you should ignore it if it tells you no.

- Should I ask this question? As in, is it okay? This is the only time you should use the word "should" in asking questions about your pendulum. Using "should" could cause your biases to affect the answers you get.

Chapter Twelve: More Magical Practices

As we wrap up this book, let's consider even more magical practices you should make a part of your daily magical life.

Consecration

Consecration involves dedicating a space or a ritual tool to a particular purpose. According to Crowley, in Magic (Book 4, chapter 13), "The ritual here in question should summarize the situation, and devote the particular arrangement to its purpose by invoking the appropriate forces. Let it be well remembered that the Oaths of its original consecration bound each object. Thus, if a pentacle has been made sacred to Venus, it cannot be used in an operation of Mars."

The very word consecration connotes "association with the sacred." You can consecrate places, things, and even people. The idea behind the practice of consecration is the devotion of what is being consecrated to one cause, deity, magical function or intention.

Evocation

Evocation should not be confused with an invocation. When you invoke, you call in a deity or a spirit. When you evoke, you call forth the entity. Crowley says, "In invocation, the macrocosm floods the consciousness. In evocation, the magician, having become the macrocosm, creates a microcosm. You invoke God into the Circle. You evoke a Spirit into the Triangle."

There are two distinct purposes for evocation. The first is to assist you in gathering information, while the second is to get the obedience or services of a demon or spirit. Seek the most effective of evocations. You will find in the grimoire on Goetia, an anonymous grimoire on demons, also known as the Lesser Key of Solomon, or the Lemegeton, or Salomonis Regis, compiled in the middle of the 17th century. This grimoire has very clear instructions on how you can safely summon the 72 infernal spirits and set them to do your bidding. You can also evoke angels, gods, and other beings with connections to the Zodiac, planets, and elements.

Magical Formulas

Magical formulas comprise a series of letters, words, or names, which have meanings that represent the magical principles and the depth of comprehension, which are difficult to communicate in any other way. These formulae offer a concise way to share abstract meanings and information using just a phrase or a word. These meanings often relate to a spiritual or mystical process of change. Some of these formulae are IAO, INRI, ShT, LVX, NOX, AUMGN, among others.

Taken at face value, these words do not mean anything in and of themselves. However, upon deconstruction, you'll find that each letter carries a universal idea within it, which is in the system the formula is based on. Also, when you group particular letters together, you can share sequences packed with meaning and are very valuable within the framework of the spiritual system they belong to.

Magical Record

The magician's magical record is a journal in which she can document all magical experiences, events, ideas, and other relevant information to her craft. Having this record can serve to keep the faith and can provide evidence about how effective a magical procedure is. It can help you make sure that all you've learned can be passed on to others long after you're gone. When you note down this information, it's easier for you to gain insights, analyze your progress, and share and learn with other practitioners like you.

For Crowley, you should keep magical records; as he notes in Liber E, you very should record all of your experiments in much detail, right after, or even during your magical performance. You want to make your records scientific and precise. Note the emotions you felt and be honest and sincere be. Note your mental and physical conditions during the experiment, the time and place, and the weather. This information will ultimately prove useful.

Magical Weapons

Magical weapons are used to create the change you seek, which conforms to your True Will. If it is your will to let everyone know what you have learned during your magical practice, then you take the weapons of pen and ink, and you write them down. Crowley acknowledges that sharing your knowledge by writing is a magical act, as is sharing the book in which you have penned your words.

Magical weapons are often very specific, and they're consecrated, and so only ever to be used in ritual or ceremonial magic. There's no rule per se about what makes up a magical weapon or what doesn't, but if you, the magus, consider an object to be a magical weapon, then for all intents and purposes, it is. However, certain magical weapons have a deeper meaning and symbolize other things. For instance, there is the athame or dagger, the holy oil, the wand, sword, oil lamp, graal, thurible, and bell, among others.

Mineral Magic

It is possible to read another's life story from just holding a bracelet of theirs. This is possible because all minerals, from crystals and metals to stones and shells, have within them the vibrations of anything and person they've been in contact with and will often hold on to all those vibrations for quite a long time.

The average person may look at minerals and think them lifeless and static, but the magus knows that you can sense energy from these metals and stones. Crystals have their own life force, as do gemstones and every other mineral of which you can think. When you imprint your intention upon a mineral object, that intention will be retained for years and years. You can also combine minerals with other things so you can strengthen your spells or lengthen how long they last.

Each gemstone has unique properties and can be used in many ways in magic. You can use them as runes, pendulums, or other tools; you can use them for healing the chakras, as a talisman or amulet, for rituals and spells, to increase meditation potency, to amplify the power of consecrated magical weapons and tools, as a gift to gods, and so on.

First, to use minerals like gemstones, wash off all old vibrations, cleansing them in salt water, and visualizing white light cleaning the stones in and out. You may combine these stones together. You can create a talisman for wealth by using tiger-eye stones, and by adding in some hematite, you make sure that whoever uses the talisman can hold on to their money.

Stones and their Magical Uses

- Amber: Protection, both physical and psychic.
- Amethyst: Enhancing meditation, dream recall, soothing emotions, enhancing psychic ability.
- Apache tears: Gives good luck.

- Aquamarine: Increases mental awareness and clarity, allows spiritual insight, boosts creativity.
- Aventurine: Attracts abundance and wealth.
- Azurite: Promotes peace and harmony, excellent for dream magic.
- Bloodstone: Gives courage, strength, healing, and physical protection.
- Carnelian: Increases sexual energy, gives initiative, courage, and boosts passion.
- Citrine: Removes and clears bad energy from other gemstones, banishes all nightmares, boosts your psychic abilities.
- Coral: Boosts feelings of affection, draws love to you, boosts your self-esteem, calms troubled emotions.
- Diamond: Builds trust and commitment, particularly in relationships. It also absorbs and retains vibrations and energies and increases chances of victory while giving strength.
- Emerald: Promotes divination and clairvoyance while boosting growth, healing, and providing emotional and mental balance.
- Fluorite: Boosts your conscious mind's strength and increases your mental skills.
- Garnet Provides protection, draws out kindness, soothes fears, and relieves all depression.
- Hematite: Perfect for grounding and centering yourself, and helps with keeping emotions stable.
- Jade: Boosts prosperity, encourages longevity, increases health and beauty.

- Jasper: Red jasper is amazing when working on love spells as it intensifies passions. Brown jasper is the stone to use for healing. The poppy jasper is best for breaking down all blocks in the body's energy circuitry.

- Lapis Lazuli: Great for children; it opens your third eye and improves your psychic abilities. It works on your higher chakras. The ancient Egyptians knew this was the stone to charge power meridians with.

- Moldavite: This improves your psychic abilities, opens your higher chakras, and speeds up the evolution of your spirit. This stone is extraterrestrial, as it resulted from a 15 million-year-old collision of a meteor with the earth.

- Moonstone: More vivid dreams, increased dream recall, and calmer emotions.

- Obsidian: Perfect for scrying, valued by Hecate, the patroness of witches.

- Onyx: Best for centering and grounding, absorbing and banishing bad energy, and destroying powerful habits.

- Opal: Improves psychic ability, protects, increases your visions, and attracts love to you.

- Pearl: Brings balance to your love life, boosts your femininity, increases your happiness and self-esteem.

- Clear Quartz: The best for retention of information, the amplification of other energies from other stones, the transmission of energy and ideas, and improved psychic awareness.

- Smoky Quartz: Holds your issues until you're ready to have them resolved, improves your endurance.

- Rose Quartz: Heals you emotionally, restores emotional balance, draws friendship and love to you, and amplifies your psychic energy.

- Ruby: Great for stimulating love, passion, and emotions, helps you open your heart to the love of the divine, and increases your vitality.

- Sapphire: Great for improving your knowledge of all things spiritual, this stone connects you with the Divine and gives you insight, wisdom, and prophetic vision. The star sapphire also gives you clarity with your True Will, and it gives you hope.

- Tiger-eye: Increases your self-confidence, which gives you the freedom to seek your own path and follow it. It's also a great stone for abundance.

- Tourmaline: The black tourmaline and green tourmaline are great for healing, cleansing, and absorbing all negative energies and vibrations. The watermelon and pink tourmaline will draw love, friendship, and fulfillment to you. You can also use them to transmit ideas, energy, and messages.

- Turquoise: This stone promotes prosperity, healing, and protection. Use it to soothe all anxiety and tension, physically and emotionally.

Here's a fact to keep in mind: Amber is not actually a stone; it is hardened resin. Lore has it that amber originally came from the tears of the sun as it set. Even now, it's still thought of as firestone or a solar stone. It's a stone most witches use to heal, as it captures all ailments and disease in the same way as it is used to capture insects.

These gemstones are typically available in many grades and qualities. You need not have a large stone for you to conduct your magic. You can simply allow your intuition to let you know the right stone that will amplify the intention you set for the ritual you're about to do.

Consider having magical jewelry made of these gems. They can prove useful for reminding you of your intentions, healing you, and serving as a talisman. Gemstones have always been connected to goddesses and gods and can even serve as offerings during your rituals. Remember that the gemstones you wear will absorb your energy, taking on some of your attributes. For instance, if you're wearing a pearl while you're joyful, it will glow. If you wear it while you feel terrible, it will go cloudy. If you're ever given a family heirloom passed down to you, you must wash it before you wear it to get rid of all unwanted, bad energy.

Conclusion

You have finally arrived at the end of this book, but you must not let your quest for knowledge stop here. It is on you, as a magus, to gather as much knowledge as you can so you can apply it to your craft and get better and better every day.

In your practice of magic, you must remember this: Do what thou wilt. Remember this is the true intent behind everything magical that you do. As you practice magic, remember that what you're doing is simply expressing your True Will in harmony with the universe. This is the only thing that matters, moment to moment.

Be aware that you must practice your craft from a place of love and compassion to all. If you choose to use your powers for evil, if you deliberately engage in magic solely to pull others down, then you must be prepared for the fact that in due time, you will receive the same treatment you've meted out, *and often a hundredfold over.*

Therefore, the wise magus knows in her practice to always remember the Golden Rule: Do unto others as you would have them do unto you. You cannot afford to be irresponsible with the knowledge you now have.

You can learn so many things in so many books about magic, but one thing trumps all books — even this one. It's the knowledge you learn from constant practice, particularly from your meditations. See to it that no matter what, you make meditation a part of your life every day. There are insights you will never glean from the page of a book; you will only experience this as you meditate, and practice Yoga and astral travel.

In your dream state, and in your astral travels, you will learn so much about the true nature of the universe, and you will receive new insight and exercises to practice to take your spiritual journey to the next level. So, you cannot afford to neglect your practice. The more you practice, the more insight you will have, and the more power you will gain.

You may notice that your exercises in this book are mostly kept as loose as possible. This is by design. To work with magical stones, do so based on your intuition. Your soul will guide you on the best methods for you to perform all rituals, from purification and banishment to blessings and divination. The thing about this magical life is that each path is unique. Therefore, you must find the path that resonates the most with you so your practice becomes something you look forward to every day.

Finally, when the supernatural begins to happen around you (and it will if you keep your practice up), please do not fall into the trap of thinking you have "arrived" at a final spiritual bus stop. There is so much more to explore. There is always more beyond where you are. Even if you learn remote viewing or be in two places at once, even if you make prophecies that come to pass no matter what, let none of that wonderful stuff stop you from practicing.

The magical journey is never-ending. Keep diving. And when you get to the bottom of the ocean, dive deeper still.

Vea más libros escritos por Mari Silva

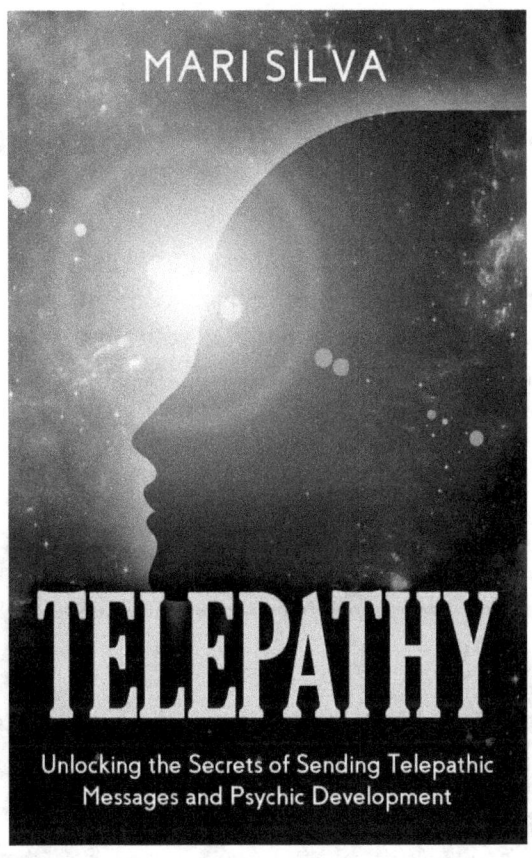

Your Free Gift (only available for a limited time)

Thanks for getting this book! If you want to learn more about various spirituality topics, then join Mari Silva's community and get a free guided meditation MP3 for awakening your third eye. This guided meditation mp3 is designed to open and strengthen ones third eye so you can experience a higher state of consciousness. Simply visit the link below the image to get started.

https://spiritualityspot.com/meditation

References

Bacon, Roger (1659, London). His Discovery of the Miracles of Art, Nature, and Magic. Faithfully translated out of Dr. Dees own Copy, by T. M. and never before in English.

Crowley, Aleister (1979), The Confessions of Aleister Crowley, Routledge & Kegan Paul

Crowley, Aleister (1985), Eight Lectures on Yoga, Falcon Press

Crowley, Aleister (1974), The Equinox of the Gods, Gordon Press

Crowley, Aleister (1997), Magic (Book 4), Weiser

Crowley, Aleister (1973), Magic Without Tears, Falcon Press